How to Use Power Phrases to Say What You Mean, Mean What You Say, and Get What You Want

Meryl Runion

D0965157

McGraw-Hill

New York   Chicago   San Francisco   Lisbon   London
Madrid   Mexico City   Milan   New Delhi   San Juan
Seoul   Singapore   Sydney   Toronto

The *McGraw·Hill* Companies

PowerPhrase is a registered trademark of Meryl Runion.

5 6 7 8 9 0   FGR/FGR   0 9 8 7 6

ISBN 0-07-142485-7

McGraw-Hill books are available at special quantity discounts to use as premiums and sales promotions, or for use in corporate training programs. For more information, please write to the Director of Special Sales, Professional Publishing, McGraw-Hill, Two Penn Plaza, New York, NY 10121-2298. Or contact your local bookstore.

 This book is printed on recycled, acid-free paper containing a minimum of 50% recycled, de-inked fiber.

Library of Congress Cataloging-in-Publication Data

Runion, Meryl.
    How to use power phrases to say what you mean, mean what you say, and get what you want / by Meryl Runion.—1st ed.
        p.   cm.
    ISBN 0–07–142485–7 (alk. paper)
    1. Oral communication.   2. Interpersonal communication.   I. Title.
    P95.R86   2004
    302.2'242—dc22   2003018280

Contents

Acknowledgments   vi

Part 1 Why PowerPhrases?
An Idea Whose Time Has Come

1. Power Up, Stand Up, SpeakStrong   3

2. PowerPhrases 101: The ABCs   12
   of PowerPhrases

3. Poison Phrases: Respect-Robbing Words   17
   That Weaken, Vicious Venom Phrases
   That Maim

4. Do You Suffer from "PowerPhrase   35
   Deficiency"? Take the PowerPhrase Quiz
   and Find Out

Part 2 The Six Secrets of PowerPhrases

5. Secret #1: It's What You Don't Say: 43
   A PowerPhrase Is Short

6. Secret #2: It's in the Details: 48
   A PowerPhrase Is Specific

7. Secret #3: Pick Winning Words That Work: 55
   PowerPhrases Are Targeted

8. Secret #4: The Power of the Simple Truth: 61
   PowerPhrases Say What You Mean

9. Secret #5: Protect the Integrity of Your 66
   Words: PowerPhrases Mean What You Say

10. Secret #6: There Is Power in Nice: 70
    Don't Be Mean When You Say It

11. A Personal Note about PowerPhrases 75

Part 3 PowerPhrases in Action

12. It Seems Like I've Known You Forever! 81
    PowerPhrases to Perfect the Connection

13. Make Your Opinion Matter: PowerPhrases 90
    to Say What You Think

14. The Secret Power of Communicating 99
    Feelings: PowerPhrases to Say What
    You Feel

15. Ask So You Will Receive: PowerPhrases to 107
    Make Powerful Requests

16. The Power of Saying NO! PowerPhrases to 116
    Refuse What You Don't Want

17. Listen So They Speak Freely: PowerPhrases 124
    to Get Them to Open Up

18. When You Really Blew It: PowerPhrases to 132
    Apologize Sincerely without Groveling

19. To Get Good Answers You Need Good 138
    Questions: Asking Questions with
    PowerPhrases

20. You Don't Have to Put Up with Put-   148
    Downs: PowerPhrase Responses to
    Unkind Criticism

21. Don't Resist Anger, Defuse It: 156
    PowerPhrases to Handle the Angry Person

22. Use Anger as a Tool, Not as a Weapon: 164
    PowerPhrases to Express Anger

23. How to Disagree without Being   175
    Disagreeable: PowerPhrases to
    Handle Disagreements

24. Homicide Is Not an Option: 185
    Use PowerPhrases to Address Issues

25. What He Says Is Not What She Hears and   193
    What She Says Is Not What He Hears:
    PowerPhrases between the Genders

**Part 4 Put Your Best Self Forward with
        PowerPhrases**

26. Tips for Using PowerPhrases   207

27. Answers to Readers' Most Pressing, Vexing, 214
    and Perplexing Communication Questions

28. Oh, My Gosh! PowerPhrases Really Work!   219
    Success Stories from the Field

29. Your PowerPhrases Final Exam   224

A Final Personal Note   239

Index   241

Acknowledgments

When my concept of PowerPhrases was embryonic, one person knew I had an important idea. Bill Cowles of SkillPath Seminars was, and remains, a source of inspiration. I figured he couldn't be wrong, so I proceeded to prove him right!

In addition to Bill, I must thank the thousands of people who have attended my seminars and those who receive my weekly newsletter (Subscribe@SpeakStrong.com). The consistent feedback I receive on how PowerPhrases work in real life provides me with insights I could not gain in any other way.

So many thanks to Bob, David, Cindi, Kjersti, Kim, Kris, Bjarni, Harriet, and everyone who has shared in my excitement each time I took a step closer to making PowerPhrases a household word.

An extra thank-you for Kris Perotsky at "A Second Pair of Eyes" for her stellar proofreading.

Why PowerPhrases?

An Idea Whose Time Has Come

1

Power Up, Stand Up, SpeakStrong

Stand up, power up, and SpeakStrong. The next time you get wind of a backstabber, address it. When your boss volunteers your department for another project, speak up about the challenges it presents and what you need to meet the challenge. When someone puts you down, tell the person how you want to be treated. When someone goes out of their way to help you, let them know exactly why you appreciate it. Take yourself off mute and speak!

But don't just speak, SpeakStrong! Speak in a way that elevates you and everyone who hears you. Speak in a way that talks the walk you want. Avoid going from silence to violence; don't go from meek and weak to rash and brash. Use PowerPhrases—winning words that work!

I hear it repeatedly. "Oh yeah, I spoke up all right. I opened my mouth and put my foot right in. Then I thought of the perfect words—AFTER it was too late." I also hear people say, "I wish I had said something, but I didn't know what to say—so I didn't open my mouth."

These people need PowerPhrases. If you ever find yourself at a loss for words, you already know why you need Power-Phrases, too. While talking is natural, talking in a way that will get you great results in today's world is not something most of us have learned. PowerPhrases is an idea whose time has come. As the amount of information we absorb increases and as our attention span decreases, it's more important than ever for you to express yourself clearly and directly. That's exactly what Pow-erPhrases will help you to do. In hundreds of situations exactly like the ones you face every day, you'll learn what words to use so that your listeners get your point.

Oh, I will give you principles. Principles are important—but principles alone are not enough. What makes *How to Use Power Phrases* different is that it provides you with the actual Power-Phrases—the exact words to embrace your message in a way that will be heard. Once you experience your meaning expressed in PowerPhrases, once you know what PowerPhrases look like, sound like, and feel like—you'll discover how to make *your* words talk the walk you want. It's time for you to SpeakStrong.

Part 1 of *How to Use Power Phrases* is about the importance of PowerPhrases and provides a basic understanding of what PowerPhrases are. Part 2 goes into depth about the PowerPhrase Principles—the secrets of what makes PowerPhrases so effective. Part 3 puts these principles in action. Part 4 ties it all together.

As unique as you are, you face the same communication challenges as everyone else. As unique as you are, you will nod with recognition when you hear the mistakes others have made, and you will appreciate the solutions offered in this book. As unique as you are, you will find yourself in every section whether you are an employee, a manager, a friend, a mother, a father, a daughter, a son—we are all people, and we need to know how to talk to each other.

How do you express yourself? Do you go from silence to violence? Do you go from being mute to being a brute? Do you go from holding back to attack? If you do, you're normal! But unfortunately, being normal comes with a price. Whether it was the wrong word at the wrong time, an unintended insult, or a moment you kept silent and wished you hadn't, I bet you have paid a price for your communication style. I bet some of the stories I'm about to tell you will trigger some not-so-delightful memories in your mind.

I want to be sure that you understand the price of silence. We'll start there. Then we'll talk about the price of speaking ineffectively. You are going to find out just why you need Power-Phrases.

Silence is golden when it's called for. Silence can be deadly when it's not called for. Don't think I'm exaggerating. Silence can cost you your promotion, your marriage, your health, your happiness—even your life.

There are four situations in which silence isn't golden:

1. Silence isn't golden when people need to know your thoughts and opinions—even if they don't want to hear them.

2. Silence isn't golden when people need to know you care.

3. Silence isn't golden when people need to be kept in the loop.

4. Silence isn't golden when people are saying or doing something that affects you negatively.

Silence Isn't Golden When They Need to Know the Truth

Where do the words you're afraid to speak get stuck? Do they get stuck in your heart without any attempt to voice them? Do they make it up as far as your throat where you choke on them? Do they get taken off your tongue by the cat?

Oh, you can hold back words that need to be spoken just like you can hold back a dog that wants to smell a hiker or a river in a rainstorm or my niece when there's a sale on shoes. You can do it for a while, but it isn't easy, and you wish you hadn't in the end.

Sheila backed off at the first sign of resistance to her words from her boss. She wished she hadn't in the end. Her boss was everything she respected in a manager and in a man—he was successful and rich. He even told her where he was going when he left the office. So Sheila had a habit of not questioning him. When he asked her to transfer funds, she expressed a tiny protest. She said,

Aren't you asking me to transfer partnership funds into a private venture?

He responded, "Sheila, are you suggesting I am asking you to do something illegal? I wouldn't do that! Now, please do what I am paying you to do."

So Sheila's hand went over her mouth. She put herself on mute and did what she was instructed. One year later, Sheila was a codefendant in a lawsuit. Sheila would have given anything to have spoken tall and used a PowerPhrase such as,

I am not willing to make this transfer until it is clear to me that this is appropriate.

Janet, a nurse in a clinic also regretted her silence. One of the doctors was everything Janet did not like in a manager and in a man. He had arrogance. He had elitism. He even had a comb-over. When Janet mentioned what she thought was wrong with one patient, her doctor-boss said, "Janet, I have a great idea. Why don't you be the nurse, and I'll be the doctor."

Janet was stunned. Janet's hand went over her mouth. She went on mute and decided not to offer any more suggestions. Two weeks later, a young man came into the office whom Janet suspected had meningitis. She kept her hand over her mouth and didn't say a word. Two days after that, the young man passed away from undiagnosed meningitis. Being right did not soothe Janet's pain. She relived the event many times, imagining that instead of cowering that she had risen up, spoken tall, and said,

I understand you prefer not to hear my opinion. I feel compelled to offer it because I suspect he has meningitis.

How about you? Whose hand is over your mouth? Who keeps you from speaking? What price have you paid for your silence? Silence is golden when called for. Silence is deadly when it's not called for. Don't think I'm exaggerating. I'm not.

Silence Isn't Golden When People Need to Know You Care

Whether it's your coworkers, your boss, your spouse, or your friends, you need to SpeakStrong with PowerPhrases and let them know what you appreciate about what they do. Hal Pitt's book *The Number One Secrets of Successful Managers* says that 85 percent of employees report that they never hear about it when they do a great job. Management is overlooking one of the least expensive and powerful motivators—acknowledgment. Don't you overlook acknowledgment as well. Stand up and say,

The reason why I appreciate what you did so much is . . .

Fill in the statement with the truth in your heart.

Silence Isn't Golden When People Need to Be Kept in the Loop

Update people on process even if you have no progress to report. Tell them,

We had ice storms that put the city in gridlock for eight hours. The shippers were delayed by two days.

They are far more likely to be understanding about why an order hasn't arrived than if you say nothing because you have no progress to report. If your boss knows that you have made three attempts to get that visa approved and are currently waiting on a return phone call, she will not nag you about not having results.

Silence Isn't Golden When Someone's Words or Deeds Affect You Negatively

I often hear about employees having long empathic discussions with each other about a coworker who overdoes the perfume, while the offender remains in the dark. Someone needs to rise up and SpeakStrong and say,

> **I am sensitive to perfumes and I get overwhelmed by yours. It gives me headaches and makes my eyes water. Would you mind toning it down?**

Take yourself off mute and SpeakStrong.

The Other Side of Speaking Tall with PowerPhrases

Taking yourself off mute is only part of what it means to SpeakStrong. If you go from being mute to being a brute, if you go from silence to violence, if you go from suppression to aggression, they will get a point, but it might not be the point you want them to get.

I see people constantly struggle to find that balance in their lives. During Patrice's performance review, the supervisor over-looked much of what Patrice had done. Patrice exploded and screamed,

This is a joke! This is unfair! You don't have a clue about what I do. You're never here anyway. You probably aren't giving me credit for what I do because it's more than you can understand.

Did Patrice think that screaming at her boss was going to enhance her ratings? In retrospect, she wished she had used a PowerPhrase and said,

Your points are well taken, and they make me aware that I have not provided you with the necessary information about my accomplishments. I believe you need that information to accurately assess my performance. Can we reschedule this meeting until a later time so I can provide you with a comprehensive picture of my accomplishments?

Then there was Robert, who responded to coworker Frank's inappropriate, unprintable hostile remarks with his own inappropriate, unprintable hostile remarks. When they met with management, Robert didn't look any better than Frank did, even though Frank had initiated the hostility.

Everywhere you turn, people are expressing themselves in ways that alienate those who can help them.

Marvin saw that happen while he waited to catch a plane to Denver. The earlier flight to Denver was boarding, and the gate agent paged two passengers. The gate agent repeated the page twice. When there was no response, she gave the seats to stand-by passengers. Apparently, the paged customers were in the area, but so engaged in conversation that they didn't hear their own names being called. When they realized they had missed their flight, they hammered the gate agent. Marvin came to her defense. "You're out of line. She paged you three times," he said. The agent assured the couple that she would do her best to get them on the next flight, which she did. Then she paged Marvin, and told him, "I gave that couple your seats. I hope you don't mind first-class." My guess is that the delayed couple would have had those first-class seats if they had spoken more effectively.

Your Balance of Power

Effective communication comes from balance—a balance of power. Your words work when you find the alternative to the pendulum of suppression-to-aggression that so many of us ride. PowerPhrases provide the essential balance necessary to truly SpeakStrong. You CAN be completely clear and completely respectful at the same time. You CAN speak powerfully without overpowering. You CAN get what you want without creating resistance and resentment. You CAN talk the walk you want. There is a middle ground, and PowerPhrases are spoken from that middle ground. Not only that, PowerPhrases don't just tell you how to approach conversations, they tell you exactly what to say.

When you hear your meaning expressed in PowerPhrases that will get you heard, you will have a sense of recognition and empowerment to be an effective player in your own life. If you relate at all to the stories I've told, take heart. There is a better way to say it, and that is what PowerPhrases are all about.

2

PowerPhrases 101

The ABCs of PowerPhrases

Have you ever had someone say something that hit you deeply and woke you into a new way of looking at things? These words shook you out of your own view, and you recognized the truth in what the person was saying. These words were "pithy"—they were full of substance and made a strong point.

I had this kind of awakening many years ago when my friend Eric was helping me fix my bike. He asked me,

Are you aware that you are coming across as condescending with me?

Whoops! He was speaking the truth and speaking it in a very clear, nonattacking, and respectful way. I hated that he was right! I hated that he was being a bigger person about it than I was. Looking back, I appreciate that he said it in a way that got through my defenses and turned my behavior around. That happened thirty years ago, and I remember it to this day. Now, that's a PowerPhrase!

Let's have a look at the definition of a PowerPhrase. The dictionary says "power" is "the ability to act or do." You have power when you can get results, make things happen, and get things done. Power is measured in outcome. The passenger who missed his flight might have felt powerful as he blasted the gate agent. In terms of results, a softer approach would have been more effective and, therefore, more powerful.

The definition of a "phrase" is a "brief expression." So a PowerPhrase is a brief expression that gets results.

Your expression needs to be targeted and worded in a way that will get results. Results come when you are specific about saying what you mean and meaning what you say, without being mean when you say it.

Therefore, I define a PowerPhrase as follows:

A PowerPhrase is a short, specific, targeted expression that says what you mean and means what you say, without being mean when you say it.

Memorize this definition! Use the definition to guide you! Ask yourself if your words are true PowerPhrases.

Let's look at the definition piece by piece.

PowerPhrases Are Short

My friend Eric's words were short. Their brevity added to their power. Passive communicators often use too many words, because they want to soften the message and water it down to avoid offending. Aggressive communicators often use too many words to intensify the message. They want to drive the message in and drive the point home. PowerPhrase communicators are simply communicating. They do not need to control the response of the listener. PowerPhrases focus on clarity. Power-Phrases are fluff-free communication.

PowerPhrases Are Specific

When Eric told me that I seemed condescending, he was specific in his choice of words. He did not just say that he didn't like the way I was talking to him. It was because his words were so specific that they had the ring of truth and hit me hard. Specific wording is like a sharp knife that cuts through defensiveness. Vague words are like cutting meat with a plastic knife.

PowerPhrases Are Targeted

Eric's words were targeted and that's why they were effective. They worked. Oh, I didn't confess to my attitude, but I got off my high horse, and have been more human with people ever since.

Target your words for the results you want. Why are you speaking? Are your goals clear in your mind? I bet you often choose words that are guaranteed to get results quite the opposite from the results you say you want.

Let's say someone is screaming at you and telling you off. My guess is that if I could put the situation on hold, pull you aside and ask what your goal in responding is, you would say,

"I want him to calm down." My guess also is that you would choose words that have the opposite effect. For example, you might want to say the words "calm down," which would inflame him even more. If your words are likely to get different results from the ones you seek, they are not PowerPhrases!

PowerPhrases Say What You Mean

What do you really mean? Have you ever told someone off in the heat of the moment and later gone back and apologized by saying, "I didn't really mean that"? You THOUGHT you meant it, but when you settled down, you realized that you were reacting to the moment, and not speaking from who you really are. Or have you ever said everything was fine, when, in fact, everything was anything but fine? Clear communication requires clarity within yourself before you can be clear with anyone else. Ask yourself, what do I really mean here?

Eric asked himself how he felt when I was talking to him. That's where he found the words to tell me that I sounded condescending.

PowerPhrases Mean What You Say

Are you willing to back your words up with action? Do you really mean what you say? If you say "I need orders by 9:00 A.M. to have them processed by 5:00 P.M.," and someone gives you an order at 11:00 A.M., do you get it processed anyway? If you say you will call, do you? Don't kid yourself—no one will take your words seriously unless you do!

PowerPhrases Are Not Mean When You Say Them

I hear your grumbling about this principle. I hear the moans and groans and the "Oh, no—you mean I can't have at them? It all sounded so doable until now!" That's right. PowerPhrases are designed to communicate without attack. Clarity without barbarity!

PowerPhrases are not venting, dumping, or unloading. Eric clearly communicated how I was coming across with him. He was in no way attacking me. He did not respond in the same condescending tone he had heard from me, and he did not use sarcasm. He was clear and direct, yet very respectful.

This means you do not get to indulge in sarcasm, mixed messages, and sideswipes! Sometimes people think PowerPhrases are the "gotcha" comments where you come across as clever and the other person cannot respond. Sorry—"I love your hair. Do you cut it yourself?" is NOT a PowerPhrase.

Now that you have all six PowerPhrases Principles—now that you know all six parts of the PowerPhrase Definition—apply all six guidelines to your words. The result will be Power-Phrases. If your words don't meet all six criteria, rethink them! It would be much easier to pick words that only meet a few of the guidelines. Easier—yes—and much less effective. Don't worry if it sounds impossible at this point. You are about to get a much deeper understanding of the PowerPhrase Principles and lots of practice in applying them to everyday situations. These six, simple elements will guide you to getting your message clearly across. But first, let's take a careful look at the words you don't want to use. Let's examine Poison Phrases.

3

Poison Phrases

Respect-Robbing Words That Weaken, Vicious Venom Phrases That Maim

Poison is something destructive or harmful. Poison Phrases are destructive, harmful phrases. Poison can either seep slowly into the system, choking off all life, or quickly kill the victim. Poison Phrases can also slowly destroy or deliver an immediate destructive blow.

There are two types of Poison Phrases. Respect-Robbing Poison Phrases weaken your own words. Vicious Venom Poison Phrases are destructive to the listener. Both kinds of Poison Phrases are the opposite of PowerPhrases. They either don't work at all, or they work in the moment and come back to bite you.

Let's begin by discussing the Respect-Robbing Poison Phrases that weaken your message. These cause others to not take you seriously.

Jana's Respect-Robbing Poison Phrases cost her credibility. "Why don't people take my ideas seriously?" Jana asked. "I've been here ten years and I know what I'm doing. People hear the same idea I offer from someone else, and talk about it like it was the greatest thing they had ever heard. When I say it, they don't pay attention." "I know exactly why they don't listen when you speak," her friend Cindi replied. "You are so tentative when you speak that no one takes you seriously. You will say, 'I don't know for sure, but I was thinking if we tried Plan A, it might work.' Then later someone else will say, 'It's obvious what we should do. Let's do A. If that doesn't work, we'll do B.' They sound certain, you sound indefinite."

"But I never know for sure," Jana responded. "No one does," Cindi replied. "Really, we're all just guessing. But you don't have to point your limitations out every time you speak!"

Jana's words were filled with Respect-Robbing Poison Phrases—words that weakened her message. More than half of the point she wanted to make was a disclaimer! *I don't know for sure, I was thinking, it might work*—it would be amazing if anyone DID take her seriously!

Let's find out what Respect-Robbing Poison Phrases find their way into your life by reviewing your personal Respect-Robbing Poison Phrases checklist.

Respect-Robbing Poison Phrases That Weaken by Playing Small

How do you limit yourself? Shall we count the ways?

1. Do you use *Filler* Respect-Robbing Poison Phrases that add no meaning, such as

Well

Um

You know

Like

Why would you ruin a perfectly powerful sentence by adding words with no meaning? Imagine a song that said, "Um, you, like, uh . . . light up my life." Those fillers would have made the difference between the hit song it was and a flop that you never would have heard of. It makes the same difference in your speech. When you use meaningless fillers, your message is weakened and your words carry less impact because the good words are diluted by your Respect-Robbing Poison Phrases.

2. Do you use *Qualifier* Respect-Robbing Poison Phrases that discount your words before they are spoken, such as

I sort of

I just

I'm wondering if

It kind of

It seems like

I could be wrong, but

This I just a thought I'm having

Sorry to bother you

I have one little question

Maybe we could

Imagine the song sounding like this:

It seems like you sort of light up my life.

No thank you! So—hello—why do you say these things in your conversations?

My assistant is a brilliant young woman who has excellent ideas. My assistant doesn't sound like she believes in her ideas. She'll say,

You may not like this idea, but . . .

or

This may not work, but . . .

If she doesn't believe in her idea, why should I? If you don't believe in your idea, why should anyone else?

I was standing next to a woman at a restaurant who also discounted her message with poison qualifiers. She placed her order like this:

I was just wondering, could I have a pepperoni pizza? And maybe a coke? I think I'd like fries too, okay?

I am not kidding, I am not exaggerating. I am not making this up! This elegantly dressed woman was asking permission to place her order! I was tempted to ask if she gives performance reviews or requests supplies the same way. Do you do that? If you do, get over it! Qualifiers dilute your message and weaken your statements and requests.

3. Do you habitually use *Tag* Respect-Robbing Poison Phrases to solicit agreement and imply that you need approval, such as,

You know?

Doesn't it?

Right?

Does that make sense?

Let's look at the song again. How would you have liked a chorus that said,

You light up my life, you know?

or

You light up my life. Does that make sense?

Quit while you're ahead! I recently heard a speaker who added "you know" after every point she made. She lost me! It sounded like she was looking for validation because she was unsure of herself. Not only that, it was irritating. I found myself listening for the "you know"s and was distracted from the message. When it comes to fillers and tag phrases, silence IS golden.

4. Then there are the *Indecisive* Respect-Robbing Poison Phrases that sound like you cannot take a stand, such as,

I should

I'll try

I might be able to

Maybe we could

You might want to consider

One possibility might be

Perhaps

Let's look at another song chorus. Instead of,

I'm gonna make you love me.

what do you think of,

I might be able to make you love me.

or

I'm gonna try to make you love me.

That sounds a lot less decisive and much less endearing!
I often hear indecisiveness when I have people set goals. If someone shares his goals by saying,

I'm going to try to . . .

or

I think I might . . .

I get tough! I tell them,

I don't want to hear about what you are going to try to do. I want to hear about what you will do.

I was looking for a title for my book and ran ideas past several people. Some people said, "I prefer title A." Others said, "I'm thinking title B is best." One woman replied,

Pick C for the following reasons . . .

I did! Her certainty sold me!

Okay. What do you say when someone asks for a report by Tuesday and you are not certain you can get it done? Don't say you'll try. Tell them DECISIVELY what you CAN do.

I will aim to complete it by Tuesday, and guarantee it by Wednesday.

Doesn't that sound stronger than

I'll try.

Think about it. When someone says,

I should lose weight.

or

Maybe we could do lunch.

do you expect action? When someone says,

I'll try to call you.

do you wait by the phone? Probably not. But, when they say,

I will lose weight.

Let's schedule lunch.

I will call you before Friday.

you believe it will happen.

5. Do you use the *Negative* Respect-Robbing Poison Phrases—the ones that can be make you sound defeated before you begin? These phrases focus on what you don't want, on what isn't working, and on what is wrong, rather than what you do want, what is working, and what is right. Some of these phrases start with

> *I'll have to*
>
> *I can't*
>
> *It doesn't*
>
> *I'm not good at*
>
> *If only*
>
> *But*

Are you depressed from hearing these words yet? When you say,

> *I'll have to . . .*

you sound like a victim. Poor you—you have to do something. Imagine if you are employed where calls need to be transferred. If you say,

> *I'll have to transfer you to customer support.*

your words imply work and imposition. If you say,

I'll be happy to transfer you to customer service.

you sound upbeat and positive. Callers will feel and hear the difference and so will you!

If you say,

I can't get this to you today.

I hear your ineffectiveness. If you say,

I can get this to you tomorrow.

I hear mastery.

If you say,

It doesn't start until 9:00 A.M.

I think there is something wrong with 9:00 A.M. If you say,

It starts at 9:00 A.M.

9:00 A.M. sounds just fine to me!

One type of Negative Respect-Robbing Phrases is the "if-only's." These are a form of "shoulda's," "woulda's," and "coulda's." These are powerless words. If only I had better letters at Scrabble or better cards in poker or if only my mommy had read to me before bed. . . . It's true, the hand you are dealt affects your choices and your chances, but you have no control over the hand you were dealt. Poison Phrases dwell on things we cannot control. PowerPhrases dwell on what we can.

6. We're not done with Respect-Robbing Poison Phrases yet! We still have the *Vague Hinting* Poison Phrases, such as,

I wish someone would . . .

when you mean,

Will you . . . ?

Hints like

I could use some help around here.

when you mean,

Please help me.

Hints like

I might want your help with . . .

to see if they pick up the hint and offer help. If what you mean is

Will you help me with . . . ?

take a deep breath and say it!

Did you see yourself in any of these weakening examples? How often have you killed your message with Respect-Robbing Poison Phrases?

Vicious Venom Poison Phrases That Overpower and Maim

I bet you have also used Poison Phrases that are too strong or that plant a bit of your venom in your listener/victim. I bet you have gone from holding back to attacking. I bet you have gone from smiling to defiling. You know why I think it's likely? Because it's part of being normal! I've done it, your neighbor has done it, your favorite boss has done it, and I bet you have, too! See if any of these Poison Phrases remind you of you.

1. Have you used Vicious Venom Poison Phrases that maim by *Labeling*? Have you ever called someone a name or expressed a judgment about someone as if your judgment was the truth? I bet you have! Watch out for anything that starts with the words "you are." Phrases such as

You're an idiot.

You're a bully.

You're selfish.

You're a bad listener.

You're cheap.

are poisonous phrases—every one. Avoid labeling! Say,

I see it differently.

I am offended by your words.

I am not getting what I need to make this worth my time.

I don't feel heard.

I need better quality.

You can say the same thing in PowerPhrases without the poison label. As soon as you label someone, he will resist or live down to your expectation.

2. Do you ever use *Absolute* Vicious Venom Poison Phrases that maim? When you speak in absolutes, you attempt to stack the deck in your favor. It might work in the short run, but in the long run it will stack against you. Avoid phrases that include

always

never

every time

everything

It is rare that someone is always late and he will resist your suggestion that he is. It is an unusual person who never is supportive. If you claim he is, you will create resistance. It is exceptional that we can say something happens every time, and usually our complaints about everything overlook some things that are appropriate. So forget the absolutes and be more specific and factual.

3. Do *Negative* Vicious Venom Poison Phrases that maim find their way into your vocabulary? Do you talk more about what you don't want than what you want? Do you talk more about what you are trying to avoid than what you are trying to create? Passive Negative Respect-Robbing Phrases that weaken

the message aren't the only kind of Negative Poison Phrases you need to watch out for. Negative Poison Phrases also can be *aggressive*. For example, watch out for

don't

no

you can't

When you say the word "don't," others hear the words that follow, the ones that tell them what you don't want and that's what gets reinforced. If you tell people,

Don't come late.

they will hear "come late." They will respond better if you say,

I need you to be on time.

The word "no" can be a PowerPhrase, but it is often used as a Poison Phrase. I saw a National Car Rental sign that said,

No Reservation, No Car.

Reservations Required.

sounds much friendlier.

When I was dropping off a car, a car rental attendant said,

You can't leave the car here!

I felt scolded. I would have been happier had she said,

Please park over there.

I saw a mother who used negative Poison Phrases to start an argument with her daughter over a toy her daughter wanted. The mother would be surprised to hear me say she started the argument, but that's what I heard. The daughter said, "Look at this toy, Mommy." Mom said,

> *You can't have it. You don't need any more toys. You have enough toys.*

"But I don't have one like this one," the child said. Mom and daughter were off and running in an argument. Why do I say Mom started the argument? The daughter hadn't said a word about wanting the toy. Mom introduced that idea. Mom was quick to point out what the daughter couldn't have, didn't need, and wouldn't get. Any self-respecting child would see that as a challenge—and many self-respecting adults would too!

4. Do you ever "should" on people? If you do, you are using Vicious Venom Poison Phrases.

I was delighted to have a few minutes to write while I waited for the airplane to finish boarding. The man sitting next to me said,

> *You shouldn't be working all the time. You should put your laptop away and enjoy the flight.*

Have you ever had someone tell you what you should do? How did you like it? People don't like you to tell them what to do even when you're right, and they hate for you to tell them what to do when you don't know what you're talking about!

I mentor a teenage at-risk boy. One day we were driving

through some lovely scenes while he studied his Pokemon cards. I said,

You should look up!

He said, "I'll look anywhere I want to!" I set myself up for that response by "shoulding" on him.

Be very careful of words like

Should

If I were you

What you need to do is

You're supposed to

You ought to

You must

People hear these words as a challenge to their judgment and as a denial of their free will. Don't tell them what to do. I could have told my young friend,

There is a great view right now you'll like.

Then he could have decided what he "should" do about it.

5. Do you ever sneak in Vicious Venom Poison Phrases that maim with *Veiled Assumptions?* Phrases that express your assumptions as facts and that draw conclusions from them are Poison Phrases. Avoid saying,

Because you didn't care enough to call, I made the decision myself.

This phrase assumes that no call came because the listener didn't care and carries on from there. Leave out the assumption and SpeakStrong by saying,

When I didn't hear from you, I made the decision myself.

Avoid saying,

If you loved me, you would get a decent job.

This remark assumes that the listener's job choice is a reflection on love or the lack of it. Instead, express the situation from your own perspective. Say,

It's important to me that you carry your weight financially.

Avoid saying,

Why do you like to make me look stupid?

That statement implies the listener gets pleasure out of making you look stupid. Instead say,

I believe what you did made me look stupid.

Address concerns directly, but don't slip them in like a Trojan Horse with another point.

6. Finally, have you ever blamed someone for something? Blame is Vicious Venom and those Poison Phrases that maim.

Blame is one of the hardest types of Poison Phrases to avoid. When you are upset with people, it's easy to assume they deserve whatever blame you lay on them. Sometimes you are right. However, if you approach them with blame, it will not be effective. Avoid saying,

> *You're not listening.*

> *You're not being clear.*

> *You don't understand.*

These phrases put the problem on the other person. Take ownership of the problem by expressing your part in it with language-phrases that start with the word "I."

Instead of

> *You're not listening.*

say,

I don't feel heard.

Instead of

> *You're not being clear.*

say,

I don't understand.

Instead of

> *You don't understand.*

say,

I don't believe I've made myself clear.

Take responsibility for your role in the situation and avoid poison blame that creates resistance.

Let's Stamp Out Poison Phrases

A dear friend and I were talking about how she likes to play devil's advocate. She discovered that people often hear her observations as complaints. She wanted to change her habit, but she was concerned that if she stopped talking the way she always has, she would have nothing left to say! That's a risk worth taking! When you stop saying things that don't work, you leave room to discover the words that do work.

Now that you know about Respect-Robbing Poison Phrases and Vicious Venom Poison Phrases, do a search to detect them in your words. Hit *delete* whenever you find them. Don't worry—you will have plenty left to say. You'll have more room in your vocabulary for PowerPhrases.

Before we move on to learning more about speaking in PowerPhrases, let's find out just how PowerPhrase proficient you already are. It's time for your first pop quiz.

4

Do You Suffer from "PowerPhrase Deficiency"?

Take the PowerPhrase Quiz and Find Out

It's time to test yourself on your level of PowerPhrase *Proficiency* and PowerPhrase *Deficiency*. Let's find out where you fall.

1. *Imagine that you joined a group for dinner and they decided to split the bill. Your tab only came to $5, and splitting the bill would cost you $70. You do not want to split the bill. What would you say?*

A) "That's outrageous! I'm not paying for your dinner."

B) "Okay, if that seems fair to you."

C) "I'm not comfortable with that because my tab only came to $5. I am comfortable chipping in $10, but no more."

2. *Your boss is unfairly critical of you at a meeting. What would you say?*

A) "You are dead wrong about that. You don't know what you're talking about."

B) Nothing.

C) "I would be very happy to discuss this issue in private. When can we meet?"

3. *Someone sent you an e-mail that said there was an attachment, but you didn't receive an attachment. What would you say?*

A) "You forgot the attachment."

B) "Gee, I'm not technical at all. I must be doing something wrong because when I try to open the attachment, I can't find one. Sorry to bother you with this, but could you resend it?"

C) "I didn't receive the attachment."

4. *Your coworker made errors in a joint report. What would you say?*

A) "This is sloppy. Obviously, you didn't proofread."

B) Nothing. You stay late to fix the errors and you don't say anything.

C) "Great job. I did find a few errors. Is now a good time for me to point them out?"

5. *You were expecting other members of your team to attend a sales meeting with you and just discovered that no one else planned to go. You do not want to handle the meeting alone and want support. What would you say?*

A) "I can't count on ANYONE here! I don't care what you have planned—you need to come to this meeting."

B) "Gee, I really don't want to go to this meeting alone."

C) "My understanding is that I would have support at this meeting. This meeting is a priority. Please come with me."

6. *A customer has a legitimate complaint, but her way of communication is offensive. She calls you a name. What would you respond?*

A) "Shut up!"

B) An apology or you say nothing.

C) "I care very much about this situation and when you speak to me this way, I find it difficult to focus on a solution."

7. *A coworker says something in a sarcastic tone. What would you say?*

A) "Whatever" in a sarcastic tone.

B) Nothing.

C) "That sounded sarcastic. Is there something we need to discuss directly?"

8. *You have a customer who seems hesitant to place an order. What would you say?*

A) "What's the hang-up? You know you want it. I've been talking to you for an hour. Come on! Quit wasting my time!"

B) "You don't want it, do you?"

C) "What concerns do you have? If we could clear those up, would you be ready to place an order?"

9. *Your coworker says, "You're not supporting me enough with this project." What would you say?*

A) "What now?"

B) "Nothing I do is ever enough."

C) "What specifically can I do to support you?"

10. *You have a teenage daughter who just got home an hour late. What would you say?*

A) "I've had it with you. You're grounded for a month. Go to your room."

B) "You don't care about me at all, do you?"

C) "I'm glad you're home safe. I was worried you were in an accident. Of course, you know what the consequences are of coming home so late. I am so relieved to see you."

Check Your Score!

If You Scored More Than 2 As:

You definitely suffer from a PowerPhrase Deficiency. You have an overload of Vicious Venom Poison Phrases that maim. I feel for the people you communicate with and it's hard on you too! Study your PowerPhrases!

If You Scored More Than 2 Bs:

Your PowerPhrase Deficiency is reflected in Respect-Robbing Poison Phrases that weaken your words. You need PowerPhrases right away!

If You Scored 8 or More Cs:

Congratulations on your PowerPhrase Proficiency. Read on to learn more.

The Six Secrets of PowerPhrases

5

Secret #1: It's What You Don't Say

A PowerPhrase Is Short

Consider this: The Lord's Prayer is only 56 words long. Do you think it would be more powerful if someone added more words? Abraham Lincoln's Gettysburg address was 226 words long. The main orator at Gettysburg, Edward Everett of Massachusetts, delivered a two-hour formal address, which Lincoln followed by speaking for two minutes. Ever heard of Edward Everett? I didn't think so. The Ten Commandments total 297 words. I think they get the point across. The *USDA Order on Cabbage Pricing* is 15,629 words long. Does that tell you anything?

Less really is more. Short really is sweet. Brief is best! If you take too long to get to the point, or worse, lose the point yourself, people's eyes glaze over, no matter how polite they are trying to be. Learn from the great communicators. Say less so your listeners understand more.

You convey purposefulness when you are concise. It shows that you have things to do, people to see, places to go. It makes what you do say all the more valuable.

Ellen discovered the value of brevity when she held the shortest staff meeting in her company's history. It lasted for three minutes. Her staff productivity soared. The other managers asked her, "What did you say?"

Ellen replied, "I told them,

We have low productivity. What are we going to do about it?

When no one spoke, I stayed silent. They squirmed, but I was silent for over a minute. I closed the meeting by saying,

This meeting is over.

They all hurried back to their desks and got things done like I've never seen before!"

In sixteen words this manager accomplished more than she had ever accomplished with hundreds of words in the past! Brevity got results!

Have you ever been at an event where you were just waiting for the speaker to shut up? Have you been to such a long meeting that to keep your sanity you had to count the tiles on the ceiling? Do you suspect people count the ceiling tiles when you speak too? Too many words weaken the impact of well-spoken words.

Remember when you were a kid and an adult started lecturing you on your misbehavior? Were you hanging on every word, eager to learn the lesson they wanted to give? I don't think so! All you could think about was getting out of there! Effective communicators don't do that. Effective communicators use brief PowerPhrases, and people hear them.

Rebecca gets to work forty-five minutes late. Her manager wants to scream or lecture her on timeliness. Instead, he simply says,

> **Rebecca, you are late and did not call. Policy requires that you notify us. I will regard this as the first time we have discussed this and make a note.**

Rebecca can whine and plead, but standing constant with this succinct statement will earn the manager more respect than a wordy assault on Rebecca's misbehavior. When you have the correct words, you don't need so many of them. Try being less wordy for a day—you will notice people's interest peak.

Recently I was watching the assistant to a CEO as she worked. Jeanette poked her head into her boss's office and said,

> *Last year we didn't use all the candles that we bought for the holiday party at the party. We had a lot left, so I brought them back to the office and used them here. Well, actually, I didn't use them all here—I did give some to Ross in marketing and Sydney in production, because we had so many. I mean they were only about half-burned. Probably not even that much. Anyway, last year we didn't have enough money for everything we wanted to get at the party. I mean, I wanted to get people goodies to take home, and there wasn't enough money in the budget for that, so we had to skip that. We also could only afford ice tea and water. So I've been trying to figure out how to save money from the holiday budget and I decided to put the candles on my budget instead of the holiday budget. Does that sound right to you?*

How did her boss ever have the attention span to listen to that woman say all that? Many people don't. Many people simply tune the other person out. Relevant details need to be there—irrelevant details need to go. Many people will tune you out at the sound of irrelevant details and miss the relevant ones! Before we move on, ask yourself what Jeanette could have said. How about the following:

> **Because we will use the leftover candles from the party in our office, I decided to put the holiday candles on my budget.**

If her boss wants more details, he can ask for them.

Have you ever gotten map directions from the Internet? They can be excellent and they can also overload you with details. Sometimes they will give five instructions just to get you on the Interstate. Once I was totally mystified by my map, and I asked a hotel clerk for directions. He said,

> **Get on the Interstate going south and take Exit 33. You'll see it from the exit.**

I followed his brief directions and found it with ease.

Celebrities, leaders, and other media-savvy people understand the principle of brevity well. If they have something they want picked up by the media, they provide statements in short catchy phrases, like

> **Count every vote.**

> **I have a dream.**

> **There is only one possible outcome here. Our victory, not theirs.**

Forgive your enemies, but remember their names.

I'll be back.

What if instead of,

I'll be back.

Arnold Schwarzenegger had said,

> *I need to go take care of a few errands—pick up some gro-ceries—put gas in the motorcycle—visit some old enemies—might take a quick nap—but listen, I should be back later—maybe a couple of hours or so, okay?*

Don't just be brief when you're *talking*. Shave your memoes, your e-mails, and your other written communications. Do you ever have people call, asking questions regarding information that was clearly stated in a memo or an e-mail? I bet the message got lost in too many words.

I will now summarize this point in two words: **Be brief.**

6

Secret #2: It's in the Details

A PowerPhrase Is Specific

"What are you looking for?" the realtor asked. Her client replied,

I don't know. But I'll know it when I see it.

The realtor had nowhere to begin.

"How do you want your steak?" the waitperson asked. The customer said,

Well done.

The steak was cooked beyond recognition.

"How do you want your hair?" the beautician asked. The woman answered,

Short.

Her hair was cut to half an inch.

The house hunter was given a run-around because he did not say,

I want a two or three bedroom house with a minimum of a half acre lot with at least two bathrooms on the west side of town.

The diner had an inedible steak because he didn't say,

I want it cooked just until the pink disappears.

The woman wore a hat for months because she didn't say,

I want soft layers about two inches long with fringed bangs.

If you aren't specific, you might get what you ask for and still not get what you want. Leave as little as possible to assumptions and interpretation.

Janice told Mark that her supervisor was undermining her. Mark knew he needed more specific information. He asked,

Exactly what is your supervisor saying or doing that leads you to believe that she is undermining you?

When Janice responded,

My manager answers questions that should be directed to me.

They then had specific information that they could use to address the problem.

Mark Twain once said, "The difference between the exact right words and the almost right words is like the difference between lightning bugs and lightning bolts." Consider the nuances of every word you speak and ask if you are speaking in the very best and most precise way.

I remember when a team member told me,

The rental car is the third car on the right.

She didn't tell me what row, so when I saw a white car just like ours, third car from the right on the first row, I locked my luggage securely inside. I missed my flight tracking down the owner of the rental car my luggage was in. Our car was third from the right in the second row. My team member wasn't specific enough and I didn't ask her to be.

Rather than say,

Write a short report.

say,

Write a 300- to 400-word report double-spaced.

Rather than say,

I need help finding my lost cat.

say,

I need your help to find my lost three-year-old silver tabby male cat who answers to the name Hank.

Rather than say,

Get this to me soon.

say,

I need this by 3:00 P.M. Thursday.

Rather than say,

Stop sexually harassing me.

say,

I want you to stop commenting on how I dress and to stop calling me honey.

And rather than say,

I hope you consider working on this project.

say,

I want you on this project with me! Your experience in process analysis is vital and nobody understands root cause like you.

And while we're on the "don't say"s, don't say anything that is considered profanity. Profanity and slang are not Power-Phrases. They are nonspecific. Their literal meaning is not what you intend at all. When you say a profane form of "forget you" is that what you literally mean? Any time you use a word that carries less of the meaning of your message, you weaken the message, even if you increase shock value. You also weaken the respect others have for you, because profanity is unprofessional.

Managers: Be specific in job requirements. I often ask my groups at seminars, "How many of you have a job description?" Usually about two-thirds of the group raise their hands. Then I ask, "How many of you have a job description that looks much like what you actually do?" Usually I have one or two hands stay up out of a room of forty or more. Don't make employees guess what their job is. Be specific.

Avoid telling employees

You are to handle administrative chores.

tell them,

> **Your job is to receive, sort, and file personnel reports monthly.**

Rather than tell them,

> *Answer the phone promptly.*

tell them,

> **The phone needs to be answered by the third ring.**

Replace,

> *You need to handle more calls.*

with,

> **I need to increase your call volume by two calls per hour.**

Parents, please do not tell young children to clean their rooms. Say,

> **I need for you to hang all the clothes that are on your chair on hangers and hang them in the closet. Then I**

need you to put the checkers in the box and put the box on the shelf. After that, line up your shoes in the closet. Then come back to me and I will tell you what to do next.

Be specific—the power is in the details.

7

Secret #3: Pick Winning Words That Work

PowerPhrases Are Targeted

All the success experts talk about it. Stephen Covey calls it "beginning with the end in mind." Lesa Heebner calls it "the Recipe for Clarity."™ Marianne Williamson calls it "Visualization." Whatever it's called, you hear it from everyone who tells you how to get what you want in life. Think of what outcome you want, and ask yourself what path of action will get you there. What could be simpler?

Well, herding cats could be simpler. Getting an election recount in Florida could be simpler. Getting your teenager to call could be simpler. But don't let that stop you. You may prefer to start talking and think later, but you won't get where you want to go if you don't know where you want to go. You must decide what results you want.

I was at a meeting of speakers before a conference when one speaker asked the meeting planner,

What do you want to be different when the conference is over? If you could wave a magic wand when the conference ends, what results do you want to see?

What a great question! He had us all focus on results. You need to do the same with your conversations.

I'm telling you to CONSCIOUSLY choose results! If your conscious mind does not chose a goal for a conversation, your unconscious mind will. Usually unconscious goals are inappropriate goals that undermine you in the long run.

Here are some common inappropriate goals:

1. To crush and destroy someone and come out triumphant (that's a little dramatic, but I bet you get my point). This goal backfires because people will get you back if you try to get them.

2. To unload and dump to relieve emotional pressure. People resist and resent being dumped on.

3. To change who someone is. That doesn't work because people change when they're ready.

4. To be right and to prove that others are wrong. This never works because everyone else wants to be right, too. The conversation becomes about who's right and has nothing to do with the issues. Being right isn't enough. Being effective is more important!

Root out your misdirected goals and replace them with conscious, workable goals. What results will work for you? Actually, there are four good goals:

1. to understand the other person

2. to express yourself so the other person understands you,

3. to problem solve, and

4. to relay needed information.

These are obtainable results that won't backfire.

Listen to people talk and guess what results they are working toward at any given moment. Better yet, ask yourself what you are trying to accomplish at any given point in your conversations. Let's look at the process by observing at a situation I once had.

My son David is a computer genius. He is my computer guru. He does not relish that role. In fact, he resists when I ask him for help. One day when David came home from work, I asked him for help with my computer as soon as he walked in the door. He immediately turned around and left without a word.

My thoughts: This kid has an attitude! After all I've done for him, is it asking too much to want a little help with the computer?

My desire: To get help with the computer and get him to clean up his attitude.

My chances of success with this agenda: Small to none.

My needed course of action: Get a better goal.

That's right. I needed to get a better, bigger goal that I could achieve. My goal was self-directed, one-sided, and likely to create resistance. So I decided that my goal would be to dissolve the tension between us concerning the computer. I guessed that would include getting my computer fixed and a change of attitude in him but I didn't assume it would.

I went to him and said,

Can we talk?

He said, "If it has anything to do with computers, go away."

This is not about me trying to get you to fix my computer.

David invited me in. I asked him,

How can we dissolve the tension between us around the computer?

His reply?

Mom, it seems like the only thing you ever come to me for is help with the computer.

BUSTED!

Here is where I could easily have become defensive and gone off track for the results I wanted. Here is where I could have changed to a goal of defending myself or a goal of blaming David or a goal of winning. Here is where I had to ask myself if I was really committed to the goal of dissolving the tension between us or if I wanted to revert to smaller goals that were likely to lead to failure. I stayed focused.

I didn't know that was an issue for you. Would you like for us to do more things together?

We started talking about all the things we could do together and our hearts opened. I had thought my son had an attitude. I did not realize that I had contributed to that attitude in a big way. When I dropped my role in David's attitude, the attitude disappeared. What a wonderful day that was. The tension dissolved into mutual appreciation.

Did attaining the goal of dissolving tension include getting my computer fixed? Well, yes, I'm happy to say that it did—on David's terms. He asked me to e-mail my computer questions to him because that is what works for him. My PowerPhrases got results.

Speaker/author Linda Larsen tells about how her son Miles stays focused on results in her audio *Power Tips*. Miles and a friend were arguing about whether a particular basketball player was right-handed or left-handed. Miles was sure he was right-handed, but the friend insisted he was left-handed. After going back and forth about it a few times, Miles said,

You may be right. He may be left-handed.

Linda asked, "How were you able to say that when you are so certain he is right-handed?"

Miles replied, "Before I take an action I ask myself,

Will the action I am about to take further the relationship or hurt it?

If the answer is that it will hurt it, I don't do it."

Wow. Miles keeps his priorities straight! Being right, proving the other person wrong—there were plenty of goals that could have overridden the goal of furthering the relationship—

but Miles decided the relationship was more important and spoke accordingly.

Before you speak, examine your words for the likely result. Saying what you mean is only a part of speaking in Power-Phrases. Being right isn't enough. Being effective is more important. The questions you ask yourself depend on your goal. Other questions might be

- **Will this remark increase their respect of me or lessen it?**

- **Will these words move us toward resolution or away from it?**

- **If I say this, will it increase the chances of me getting what I want or decrease it?**

Say what you mean when you speak, but choose the words to say it that result in a positive outcome. If what you are doing isn't working, change your approach! You might think your approach should work—but if it doesn't, give it up!

Before you speak, ask yourself what your thoughts are, what your goals are, what your chances of success are, and what results you might be better off pursuing.

8

Secret #4: The Power of the Simple Truth

PowerPhrases Say What You Mean

When a politician answers "No comment" to a question posed by a reporter, chances are if he or she were more honest, the response would have been, "I haven't decided what my opinion is. I haven't read the polls yet." Politicians are often accused of saying what their constituents want to hear and not saying what they mean. Many people have suggested that Al Gore lost the 2000 presidential election because he changed his positions on issues based on polls of voters.

Politicians aren't the only ones who do this. There is a joke about an employer who interviewed several accountants by asking, "What is one plus two?" The candidate who got the job was the one who answered, "What do you want it to be?"

You do need to consider how your words will be interpreted. But don't be so concerned with how others will respond that you lose your own truth. When you do that, you lose authenticity. Without authenticity you have no power.

In the year 2001, Secretary of Defense Donald Rumsfeld became famous for speaking simply. When asked a question he didn't want to answer, he would say,

I could answer that, but I won't.

In a political world where no one puts their cards on the table, people found Rumsfeld's straightforwardness refreshing. The press loved him even though he maintained absolute control of every press conference.

So ask yourself—What do you really mean? When you said to a coworker,

I wish I didn't have to go to this meeting alone.

was that what you meant? Or did you mean,

Please come to the meeting with me.

but you didn't want to say that because you were afraid of imposing on her time?

When you said,

This printer is lousy.

Did you really mean,

I need you to requisition a new printer for me.

but you were afraid to ask directly because you were afraid she would get upset? Then did you get upset when the printer you never asked for never came?

Travis didn't say what he meant to his boss. Travis's boss called him into his office and then kept Travis waiting for fifteen minutes while he discussed social matters with someone on the phone. Travis's coworker, Brent, never had that happen. The boss asked Travis if he minded waiting. Travis said,

No problem.

But he did mind. When he said, "No problem," he was thinking about all the work that was waiting for him at his desk. He felt awkward and humiliated standing there while his boss joked on the phone about tennis scores. He wished he could leave, and he didn't know whether he should sit or stand, or pretend he wasn't listening. A day earlier, when Brent was faced with a similar situation, he simply said,

I need to get some work done while I wait for you. I'll check back in a few minutes.

Brent said what he meant and he followed through. Brent earned his boss' respect and Travis did not. Also, Brent is "training" his boss to be attentive to him when he comes into the office; Travis is allowing himself to be devalued as an employee with nothing better to do.

I've shared some examples of situations where speakers watered down their meanings with Respect-Robbing Poison Phrases. That's not the only way we avoid the truth. Sometimes we over-dramatize with Vicious Venom Poison Phrases.

My friend Shelly called me in a panic because her partner

Vince threatened to quit. I knew that would never happen. He wasn't saying what he really meant. When he said,

> *I should never have agreed to this partnership. I hate working with you. I quit.*

what he meant was

> **I am frustrated by your resistance to my new ideas. I want you to hear me out and consider how my ideas could work before you start telling me why they won't.**

I know that's what he meant because that's the truth they got to after days of fighting and hurt feelings.

Self-knowledge is essential. You have to ask yourself—What do I REALLY mean? Clear communication requires clarity within yourself before you can be clear with others. Ask yourself for the simple truth and I mean the BIGGER simple truth. You must ask yourself three essential questions.

1. What do I think?

2. What do I feel?

3. What do I want?

Here's the hard part. You MUST tell yourself the truth. In my experience working with clients, the most difficult part of identifying what you mean is to know what you feel. People will say, "I feel . . ." and follow it with a thought.

> *I feel you don't love me.*

I feel that you are harsh.

I feel that you could get the answers for yourself without interrupting me.

None of those are feeling. They are thoughts. Feelings in these situations could be

I feel ignored.

I feel attacked.

I feel frustrated.

Somewhere in what you tell yourself are the words that you can tell someone else for results. You take a risk when you open up and express what you really mean and allow yourself to be vulnerable. Where you risk most is where you stand to gain most. Are you willing to risk saying what you really mean in your mind and in your heart?

This week let someone know what you really mean. Don't look to the polls for your answers. Tell them what you think, feel, and want. Speak your simple truth.

9

Secret #5: Protect the Integrity of Your Words

PowerPhrases Mean What You Say

Carina had it with her coworker, Grace. She was so tired of listening to Grace complain about how overworked she was that she decided to SpeakStrong. She said,

> **Grace, I won't listen to you complain about your workload anymore. I want you to bring those issues somewhere else.**

How much power is there in Carina's words? That depends on Carina. Carina doesn't need to convince Grace that she is wrong to complain about her workload for Carina's words to be powerful. Carina doesn't need to convince Grace that she is right to stop listening. What she does need to do is to refuse to listen the next time Grace starts to complain about her workload to her. If Carina says she won't listen, she needs to mean it.

The flip side of saying what you mean is to mean what you say. That means you back your words up with actions. Your words are as powerful as your commitment to them.

In a previous chapter, I talked about Vince who threatened his partner with quitting. I told you Vince didn't really mean what he said. The reason I knew Vince didn't really mean it was because he had made many idle threats throughout his years of working with Shelly. He has a history of saying things he doesn't mean and so his words have lost power. Your word is your bond and you must respect your own words if you want anyone else to.

People respect people who do what they say. If you do not respect your own words, what makes you think anyone else will? If you don't mean it, don't say it. Avoid saying,

I'll be there at 3:00 P.M.

and then show up at 4:00 P.M. Avoid saying,

The check's in the mail.

if it isn't. Avoid saying,

I can't talk right now.

and then stay on the line for ten minutes. If you do not back your words up with action, you teach people your words have no meaning. You lose their respect.

Parents do this all the time. Do you know children who only respond when their parents yell? They do this because their parents yell when they finally mean what they say. Children know that until the parent yells, the words are empty. Coworkers, bosses, and employees also recognize empty words. Protect the power of your words—**if you don't mean it, don't say it!** You train other adults the same way parents train children.

Everyone shows up to Roger's meetings on time because when he says,

The meeting starts at 9:00 A.M.

it does!

People get their typing to Bill on time because when Bill says,

I need this by 10:00 A.M. to get it out today.

they know that if they get it to him by 10:30 A.M., they are taking their chances of having to wait until tomorrow.

If Mary says,

I'll call you at 2:00 P.M.

Victoria waits near the phone at 2:00 P.M. because she knows the call will come.

The next time you promise a customer that it will be done in an hour, have it done in an hour. If you aren't certain you can get it done by then, say,

I'll get it to you in two hours.

The next time your boss wants you to finish an impossible workload by quitting time, assess if you can achieve it with quality, and if not, say,

In order to do a quality job, I will need until noon tomorrow to complete this.

Never promise what you can't deliver, never agree to something you have no intention of doing, and never commit to anything you aren't 100 percent committed to accomplishing.

Think about how advertisers lose credibility by not meaning what they say. How many "final markdowns" will you accept? How many one-day-only sales will you be motivated by? You know if you miss this sale you will catch the next one.

How about politicians who promise anything to get the election, and find they cannot deliver? I'm sure the senior George Bush squirmed each time clips of him saying, "Read my lips: No new taxes" were aired after he had gone back on that campaign promise. Many people say it cost him his second term.

Take your words seriously so other people will.

10

Secret #6: There Is Power in Nice

Don't Be Mean When You Say It

I helped a client draft a "Power Letter" to get a former client of hers to make a payment that he owed her. The letter was clear and firm. It closed with, "I wish you the best." My client said, "I'd rather say: Just pay up, you slime ball!"

I asked, "How effective do you think that would be?" She then asked me, "Should I say it if I don't mean it?" I told her no, but asked, "Is there any part of your heart that wishes him well? If you can find some respect in your heart and communicate that, I believe your chances are greater of succeeding."

The client modified my recommended closing to words of well-wishing that more closely matched what she could find in her heart. After she sent it, she was glad she had included that. The letter was well-received and successful.

When someone hurts you, human nature is to want to hurt them back. You need to tell the truth about that to yourself, because if you keep this desire unconscious, it is more likely to slip into your words and into your actions. You will go from being mute to being brutal, from suppression to aggression, from silence to violence. You might not recognize it in yourself, but others will. You cannot SpeakStrong when you unconsciously seek revenge. Listeners will hear Poison Phrases and resist.

PowerPhrases respect the other person, even if that person is not respecting you. In my PowerPhrase seminars, I give students carefully prepared real-world problems and ask the group to find the words to address the issues. I begin by instructing, "Choose your words so that your listener will leave ready to make a change and give you what you want. But also choose your words so your listener leaves feeling better about themselves and better about you than they did when they came in." That's when everyone groans. The second goal makes it harder to figure out what to say; yet it is worth the trouble. Your words will carry more power and will win you respect.

When I tell you, "Don't be mean when you say it," what kinds of "meanness" do you need to watch out for?

Watch out for blame. Take this next guideline to heart— ELIMINATE BLAME! Yep, eliminate it! You can—and you must—let people know what you think, feel, and want with NO BLAME AT ALL!

For example, instead of saying,

You are vicious.

say,

I am offended by your remark.

Instead of saying,

You are not making a bit of sense.

say,

I don't understand.

Instead of saying,

You're not paying attention.

say,

I don't feel heard.

Do you see what these Poison Phrases have in common? They begin with the word "you." Watch yourself next time you start a sentence with "you." There is a very good chance you will follow with blame. Instead of blame, factually describe the situation from the perspective of what you think, feel, and want.

This is difficult because when you are upset with people you believe they are to blame. They are vicious, they aren't making sense, they aren't paying attention—so why can't you tell it like it is?

The answer is that your judgments aren't reality. Your judgments are the story you tell yourself about reality. When you communicate your judgments, you trigger their defensiveness.

There are three stories—yours, theirs, and the facts. By the facts I mean the story a neutral party would tell.

When my computer-genius son refused to help with my computer, my story was

David has an attitude.

His story would probably have been something like

> *My mom doesn't respect me and just wants to use me to fix her computer.*

A neutral story would be

> **We had different expectations about David's role in fixing my computer and it was creating tension.**

The neutral story says what you mean without blame.

Another way of being mean is to use sideswipes, hit and run tactics, mixed messages, and sarcasm. These tactics can be so hard to see! One woman looked absolutely innocent when she told me about how she was offended by the backstabbing at meetings. So she wrote down the meeting minutes verbatim— including every dig, sideswipe, and insult. "Now everyone is mad at me!" she said. "I was just trying to get them to stop!" Don't kid yourself! I don't care if you fully believe they deserve it, these tactics have no place.

Avoid hit and run tactics, like saying,

> *Late again?*

and then walking off.

Resist the temptation to say,

> *I'm surprised you noticed my attendance since you're hardly ever here.*

Refrain from saying,

Great job. Who helped?

What is the intent behind these remarks? The purpose is to stick the knife in without allowing listeners to stick it back to you. The purpose is to spread the poison of your venom without being accountable.

The only place for sarcasm is when you have a high degree of trust and goodwill and your listener knows there is no malice intended.

Another way of being mean is to use words that are stronger than needed. Start speaking by giving your listeners the benefit of a doubt and strengthen your words as you need to.

When you pick your words, create two goals. One goal will be for what you want listeners to do. A second goal will be a relationship goal. How do you want the relationship to look when all is said and done? Does having two goals make finding the perfect words harder? You bet! It makes it harder—and so much more effective.

You can find alternatives to silence other than violence. The alternative to holding back is not to attack. Keep your poison to yourself and SpeakStrong, without being mean when you speak.

11

A Personal Note about PowerPhrases

Sometimes people ask me—Have you always been so articulate? They seem to think that I was born with a silver PowerPhrase in my mouth. I wasn't. I have paid enormous prices for my silence and for speaking small. I have also paid a price for spreading venom. That is why I am so passionate about PowerPhrases.

I had a huge wake-up call that taught me that I *needed* to become more expressive. It happened in 1985 when my husband, Mike, became ill, and I suspected he had cancer. When I told him, he screamed at me for suggesting the possibility. He said, "Damn it, Meryl, I don't have cancer—and don't mention it to me again." I put myself on mute as I watched my husband fade away day-by-day. I cannot describe how painful it was. Mike passed away on May 13, 1986, from colon cancer.

I believe that his cancer may have been treatable the day I first mentioned it to him. I don't assume he would still be with me if I knew then what I know now about communication, but I do believe it is possible. I dropped the ball and we both paid the price. I lost Mike, and I also lost myself in the process by not speaking my truth.

A few months after Mike's passing, as I was sitting in a counselor's office, the counselor asked me, "Whose hand is that over your mouth? Who is keeping you from speaking?"

I was shocked to realize that I had my hand over my mouth in a gesture that said, "I must not speak." I was keeping *myself* from speaking. It was not Mike's hand over my mouth, it was my own. My responsibility to myself and everyone else in my life was to get my hand off my mouth and find my voice.

Unlike in school when you fail a test, in life you often get to do a retake. I got to take a test again about six months after Mike's passing.

I was on lunch break from a CPR class. When I went to a grocery store, in the parking lot a group of people was standing around an unconscious man. I wondered whether he had had a heart attack. Maybe he needs CPR. I'm half-trained!

But once again I was afraid to speak. Once again, when my first attempt to communicate was not heeded, my hand went up over my mouth. I said in a feeble little voice, "Maybe he needs CPR." When no one paid attention to me, I went right back on mute. When the ambulance finally came, my personal test was over, and once again I had failed.

I was sick at heart for days. I became even more painfully aware of how costly my passiveness was. My commitment to find my voice became stronger. I picked myself back up and I redoubled my efforts to take that hand off my mouth and to stand tall and SpeakStrong.

I did what many people did. I went from mute to brutal. My first attempts to give myself a voice were not pretty. I used every Poison Phrase that exists, alienating a lot of people. Eventually, I did find the middle ground.

Have you been tested with situations that called for you to SpeakStrong? How did you do? If the answer is not too well, listen carefully. Life will test you again.

Part 3

PowerPhrases in Action

12

It Seems Like I've Known You Forever!

PowerPhrases to Perfect the Connection

Everyone in the room wanted to speak at once. Their feelings were intense, their passion aroused, their opinions deeply engrained. What was the topic at this communications seminar that aroused such fervor? Small talk!

"It's trivial!" "It's a waste of time!" "It's boring!" "Empty!" "Shallow!"

I stood firm against the onslaught of resistance. Small talk may be all of these things. Small talk is also necessary—and you need to master it!

Does this sound familiar to you?

You've just met someone new. You decide to strike up a conversation. You ask the person, "How are you?" and he responds with, "I'm fine. How are you?" Now it's your turn. You say, "I'm fine."

If this person has something you want, you have just missed an opportunity.

Think about the important relationships in your life. Didn't they begin with small talk? Think about the important conversations in your life. Didn't they begin with small talk? As Deb Fine says in *The Fine Art of Small Talk*, big things begin with small talk.

So how do you get a conversation going if all you have to go on is a simple "How are you?" Use PowerPhrases to perfect the connection. Let's take a look at how the PowerPhrase principles apply to small talk. Remember, a PowerPhrase is a short, specific, targeted expression that says what you mean and means what you say without being mean when you say it.

PowerPhrases to Perfect the Connection Are Short

I confess I recently opened a conversation with a banquets manager with the standard and not very inspiring, "How are you?" When I say our PowerPhrases ought to be short, that's a bit too short!

To my surprise and delight, the banquets manager told me exactly how she was doing. She replied,

I'm great because it's almost the weekend and I love my weekends!

Her response was short, but it was long enough to give me something to work with. My question was a simple question that usually does little to get a conversation going. But her reply got our conversation up and running. I was now able to ask her for more information. She had invited me into her world! Now I could ask,

Why do you love weekends? Tell me your secret!

Fishing? What do you love about that?

Camping? Oh, I know a great camping spot.

Do you see what she did? She gave a little extra information, which gave me material to work with. Understand, you do not need to use a lot of words—you can do it in one sentence!

The next time someone you just met asks, "How are you?" give them a little extra information. Let that person know that you appreciate them asking. Try something like

Excellent, because I got my hike in this morning.

A little sad because my son is moving out.

Excited because I go on vacation tomorrow.

Now, please note, I said a LITTLE extra information. When I'm checking out my "6 items or less" at the supermarket, and I ask the cashier how she's doing, I'm not looking for,

I'm just so glad it's Friday because I haven't had a day off in 5 days. And I've been here since 7:00 A.M. and I still haven't had a break—and it should be my lunchtime but since there's no one else to cover the register. . . .

Sometimes people are looking for just a simple "I'm fine." So keep your response short, but long enough to invite them into your world. While they may be surprised when you tell them about the great deal you just got on your new shoes, you might just make a new friend. If they are interested in getting to know you, they certainly will welcome the gift of a little extra information.

Give a little extra information and give the listener room to respond.

PowerPhrases to Perfect the Connection Are Specific

I understand why some people find small talk so boring. Often it is the exchange of empty phrases with very little meaning and don't hold interest at all. We habitually put on a social face and leave ourselves at home. But it doesn't have to be that way! You can be creative and specific and learn something you didn't know from someone you met two minutes ago.

The man sitting next to me on an airplane was looking through a toy catalog and tore out a few pages of the ads. I noticed some were girls' toys and some were for boys, so I asked,

You've got a girl and a boy?

He replied,

I have a girl and three boys, but I also work for a toy manufacturer.

The conversation that followed was interesting and specific. It was not a conversation I could have had with just anyone. It was the unique nature of it that made it both satisfying and rewarding.

I was specific when I asked a banquets worker,

You look full of joy. What's your secret?

I had observed him and based my conversation on what I noticed. He was delighted to tell me why he was so happy. Pay attention to people. The key to getting the conversation going could be right in front of your eyes.

Many people wear T-shirts with the company logo these days. What can you say about that? Is the person across from you holding a book? What is it? What would you like to know about it?

Pay attention to your thoughts. The key to getting a conversation going could be hidden in those thoughts. When you share your thoughts, you open the conversation up. If you notice yourself wondering if the person standing next to you knows what the stock market did that day, ask them! You don't have to limit your small talk to a generic discussion of the weather.

PowerPhrases to Perfect the Connection Are Targeted

Ask yourself what your goals are before you go to an event where you will be connecting with people. Make sure your phrases meet your goals. Are you there to have fun? Pick subjects you enjoy talking about.

I'm looking for a good movie. Got any recommendations?

What do you do to relax?

Are you there to take business cards? Talk about business.

What do you enjoy about your job?

I'm in the publishing industry. How about you?

Are you there to establish friendships? Make your focus more personal. Say,

Tell me about your family.

That's a lovely necklace. Is there a story behind it?

Are you there to learn whatever these people can teach you? Ask,

What would you recommend to someone who has never been here before?

What did you do before you worked here?

Notice that the above questions are all open ended— meaning they require more than a one-word answer. Were you to say,

Do you enjoy your job?

Do you have a family?

Some weather, huh!

you'll get a "yes" or "no." That gives you nothing to work with. If you ask too many closed questions, you'll sound like a detective. I want you to be a detective to find their hidden treasures, but I don't want you to sound like a detective. I want you to get results.

PowerPhrases to Perfect the Connection Say What You Mean

What is the invisible barrier we put between ourselves and people we don't know? It's as if we think we need to put on a mask and pretend. Don't pretend you are someone you're not. But do pretend you know them already.

What would you say to this person if you already knew them? No. I'm not suggesting that you open a conversation with a stranger by saying,

> *I just had my warts removed and they're growing back again. Has that ever happened to you?*

or

> *My mom is in a drug rehab program. Do you have any experience with them?*

What I am saying is that you probably have artificial barriers with people you don't know. You edit things that would be perfectly appropriate to say because "you don't know them." So go ahead and say,

This song reminds me of when I lived in France.

if that's what comes to mind, or

> I love that flocked Christmas tree. It reminds me of one
> I had as a child.

if that's what you would say if you already knew them.

In my first phone conversation with my editor at McGraw-Hill, we dropped the barriers and were playful with each other from the very beginning. It was after 5:00 P.M. his time on a Friday, and I asked if he always worked that late or if he was waiting for my call. He said,

> I stayed later tonight because I had a hot new author to
> talk to.

The flattery wasn't wasted on me, but the playfulness is what made me think "I want to work with this man." I had a flavor of what he was like and what it would be like to work with him within minutes of starting the conversation because he didn't wear his "stranger" mask. Act at ease with people you don't know, even if you're not. Be yourself and look for hints about what to say in your own thought processes.

The formula is simple: Ask yourself what you would say if you already knew this person. Review what you think, feel, and want. Then ask yourself if expressing any of that will achieve your goals.

PowerPhrases to Perfect the Connection Mean What You Say

Often when people are making new acquaintances, there is a tendency to want to look good and to say whatever you believe they want to hear. You must be genuine from the start, and only say what you expect you will follow through with. Don't say,

I'll call you.

if you mean you're going to shred their card. Don't say,

I have five degrees.

if one is elementary school, one is junior high, and one is high school.

PowerPhrases use "truth in advertising." You never know when you will run into these people again and in what other ways your paths will cross. Mean what you say—speak the truth.

PowerPhrases to Perfect the Connection Are Not Mean When You Say Them

While I suggest that you drop artificial barriers, I also suggest you tread lightly on potentially sensitive areas—particularly religion, politics, and sex. Be sure enough trust is there before you poke fun. They don't know you well enough to understand how to take your comments or when you are joking or serious.

13

Make Your Opinion Matter

PowerPhrases to Say What You Think

Everyone has one. Everyone thinks his is the best. Everyone wants other people to pay attention to hers. So how do you get anyone to care about yours? I'm talking about opinions.

A mythical character named Cassandra was given the gift of prophecy. She could clearly see the future. Unfortunately, she was not also given the gift of persuasion. She knew what she was talking about, but no one believed her. Her knowledge was useless. Do you ever feel like Cassandra?

I'm sure Temple Grandin did. She was part of a design team that created a new processing system for a meat-packing plant. Temple, being exceptionally visual, pictured the entire process from beginning to end. She clearly knew that the way the system was designed could not possibly work. Unfortunately, her verbal skills did not match her visual gifts. Her team not only ignored her warnings, but also she was fired when she persisted. On the first day of operation, the system collapsed, taking the ceiling with it. Temple knew this would happen, but no one believed her. That made her knowledge useless. Do you ever feel like Temple?

I've often wondered how the Research and Development people at IBM felt when they developed graphic interfaces and the mouse yet couldn't convince management to produce it. Not only that, they were ordered to hand their invention over to Steve Jobs at Apple computers. Do you know what Steve's net worth is today? $1.4 billion.

Being right isn't enough! Knowing what you are talking about isn't enough. You also must know how to communicate your thoughts.

To make your opinion matter, you need to say what you think in PowerPhrases! Short, specific, targeted expressions that say what you mean and mean what you say, without being mean when you say them.

PowerPhrases to Say What You Think Are Short

Do not give the entire history of thought behind your opinions. Rather than saying,

This is the best proposal because of the following 47 reasons, which I will now elaborate in excruciating detail based on my analysis of Plato, Aristotle, moving forward to John Nash.

say,

This is the best proposal because it will increase our margins by 32 percent and carries the lowest initial outlay. I have documentation for your review.

Summaries with supportive documentation are effective. If people don't begin to understand something after a quick review, they often won't look any further. While you may find every detail fascinating, it doesn't mean they will.

Simple main points are most easily grasped. I have had many people tell me that the best thing they take with them from my seminars is the reminder to

Say what you mean and mean what you say without being mean when you say it.

My seminars are packed with tools and information, but it is the simplicity of that one statement that makes my point so they get my point.

PowerPhrases to Say What You Think Are Specific

Don't just say what you think, give brief reasons to support your opinion. Rather than saying,

This vendor is best.

say,

This vendor is our best choice because they have a 10 percent shorter turnaround time and a 30 percent

higher response rate for only 2 percent higher cost than the nearest competitor.

Avoid saying,

$14.95 is too low a price.

say,

If we price it at $14.95, the reps won't make enough in commission to be willing to promote it.

Don't say,

This article is too long.

say,

The average article is 400 to 600 words. This one is 1,100 words. We need to edit it down to appeal to the average attention span.

Throughout this book, I express what I think and then back up my assertions with specific examples and illustrations. I don't just tell you it's important to be able to communicate your ideas effectively, I also provide illustrations of what happened to people who didn't. I let you experience for yourself why my ideas are valid when I demonstrate what not to say and follow it by what to say instead. Do you want to convince someone of something? Give examples and be specific.

PowerPhrases to Say What You Think Are Targeted

The perfect words to get your point across depend on your goal. What do you want to happen?

- Is your goal to get them to buy into your idea?

- Do you simply want them to consider your idea?

- Are you trying to start a discussion based on your idea?

Pick an approach that will get your desired results. If you want people to buy-in, speak decisively. If you want them to consider your idea, let them know this is your opinion. If you want to start a discussion, tell them you are sharing your ideas to start a discussion.

It is rare to be 100 percent sure of anything. Don't wait until you have absolute certainty to speak decisively.

Throughout this manuscript I have edited words such as "I believe," "I recommend," and "It seems to me." I want you to take my words seriously, so I avoid qualifiers. For example, in my previous chapter I started to say,

I believe small talk makes big things happen.

I edited it to say,

Small talk makes big things happen.

Doesn't that sound more powerful? To state my knowledge as belief limits the impact.

If you want your ideas to be taken seriously, state them without qualifiers. Avoid saying,

> *I think you are scheduled to start at 9:00 A.M. and it looks like you have come in at 9:25 A.M. four out of five days this week.*

Say,

> **You are scheduled to come in at 9:00 A.M., and you have come in at 9:25 A.M. four out of five days.**

Use the words "I think," "I believe," and "My opinion is" only if

1. You have a reasonable doubt.

2. The person you are speaking to is threatened by such strong wording—particularly when the conversation is getting sensitive.

3. You are looking for discussion rather than buy-in.

Otherwise state your opinion and let it stand.

PowerPhrases to Express Opinions Say What You Mean

In order to be clear in expressing opinions, you need to be clear within your self. What do you really think? What do you really mean?

When Kathy's boss wanted to introduce mandatory drug testing, Kathy feared for the company. She knew that half of the staff would be offended and the other half would need to be replaced. Kathy understood the culture of the company better than the CEO did. In communicating her opinion, Kathy forgot all that and spoke indirectly. Instead of saying what she meant, she asked her boss,

Are you sure you want to do that?

Her manager said, "Yes, absolutely." Kathy went on to say,

I wonder if the employees will be happy about it.

Her manager replied, "They don't have to like it—they just need to be drug-free." Kathy continued to dance around her point. She said,

I'm not sure it's a good idea.

Her boss put her pen down and said,

Kathy, what do you mean? What are you trying to tell me?

Finally Kathy Spoke Tall and said,

I see serious risks in that action. I think you don't know the culture here. I estimate that half the staff won't pass the test. The other half will be offended. Instead of doing across the board testing, it will be less disruptive if we implement testing on an as-needed-basis.

Kathy's recommendations were adopted.

PowerPhrases to Say What You Think Mean What You Say

Do you walk your talk? No one will believe you if you do not live what you say. One insurance salesman was frustrated by his inability to sell large life insurance policies. A coworker pointed out that the salesman himself did not have a large life insurance policy, so his recommendations lacked credibility.

PowerPhrases to Say What You Think Are Not Mean When You Say Them

Be certain to consider your listeners. Be careful not to criticize any opposing ideas or to imply that they must be crazy if they do not buy into your idea the way you want them to. Avoid the phrases

Anyone would know

It should be obvious to you

As anyone can see

Those phrases create defensiveness.

Also, do not communicate judgment thoughts, blame, or thoughts that put-down your listener. When you are tempted to blame, express your thoughts without blame.

In some cases you will want to tone down the strength of your opinions by adding the phrases

I believe

I recommend

My opinion is

These phrases dilute the strength of your message somewhat, and should only be added when your listeners are more likely to be receptive to a softer message.

If you want to be listened to, be very clear about what you think and about the PowerPhrases that will get you heard.

14

The Secret Power of Communicating Feelings

PowerPhrases to Say
What You Feel

"We don't cry or lose our temper because we express our feelings too often but because we express them too rarely."
—*Difficult Conversations*,
Douglas Stone, Bruce Patterson, Sheila Heen

In my experience teaching seminars around the world, I have learned that feelings are one of the hardest things for people to communicate. People often speak *from* feelings, but it is far more difficult for them to speak *about* feelings. Hey—I can relate! I used to spend an entire hour with my counselor pressuring me to identify and express a single feeling before I would admit to feeling anything.

This is not unusual. Many people don't know what they

feel. Many people are afraid to admit they feel. Many people are emotionally constipated.

In my seminars I ask people to tell a partner what they think, feel, and want about a situation. They usually do well on the thoughts and wants, but the vast majority flunk feelings. And yet feelings are an important part of every communication. Often, feelings are what the communication is about. When feelings are essential to the message, feelings are where the power is.

So admit what you feel in short, specific, targeted expressions that say what you mean and mean what you say, without being mean when you say them.

PowerPhrases to Say What You Feel Are Short

Do not go into a lot of detail about what you feel, do not over-explain your feelings and do not justify your feelings. Instead of saying,

> *When I was growing up, my mother would make crazy statements and I would try to point out why they were ridiculous and she would resist and insist they were true and I felt so helpless and felt a great need to show her how right I was and how wrong she was. Then when I was . . . which is why when you say something that doesn't make sense to me and won't discuss it, it brings me back to those days and I feel frustrated and confused and angry and . . .*

Just say,

I feel frustrated and confused.

If you are in therapy, go into great detail about what you are feeling. In most conversations, a simple sentence or two will serve you better. Be brief instead.

People are often reluctant to communicate feelings because they are afraid of sounding too emotional. When you keep your mention of emotions short, it actually creates a balance to the rest of your message.

PowerPhrases to Say What You Feel Are Specific

When you talk about feelings, express specific emotions. Tell them you are frustrated, annoyed, elated, and exhausted. Let them know when you are overwhelmed, concerned, frantic, or serene. Avoid expressing judgments that are disguised as feelings. If you say,

I feel like you're an idiot.

I feel this isn't right.

I feel you mistreated me.

Your words communicate thoughts not feelings. When you express a thought as a feeling, it creates confusion. When you express the specific feelings behind the thoughts, it adds power to your message.

There is a tendency in our culture to use general words to

describe emotions that do not provide much information. Often people say they are angry, when if they looked more deeply they would realize that they felt much more than simple anger. Don't say you're mad when you are offended, baffled, and irate. Be more specific. It strengthens your message.

I was feeling frustrated with my assistants, but wanted to be certain I was being specific in my words. I looked more carefully and realized what I was really feeling was something different. I said,

I feel out of touch with both of you.

By describing what I really felt, it was easier to know what to do about it! It often makes it easier to hear, which was certainly true in this case.

PowerPhrases to Say What You Feel Are Targeted

You feel so many things. Which feelings do you believe will get the result you want with the listener? If someone stands you up for an appointment, and you are angry, frustrated, offended, and surprised, which feeling do you believe they will respond to best? Remember—a PowerPhrase is as strong as it needs to be and not stronger. Ask yourself which emotions most closely match the situation and will work for the results you seek.

There are situations where you might choose to omit your feelings; however, in far more situations they will improve your results.

For example, imagine I interrupt you while you are working and my interruptions frustrate you. If your message to me is

You will save yourself time if you ask me all your questions at once.

I won't understand that I am creating a problem for you. I might not stop. Say,

The interruptions frustrate me.

I need to know exactly why you want me to stop interrupting you.

If your jokes offend me, and I say,

You might not want to tell that joke anymore.

you won't understand and are less likely to stop than if I say,

Ouch. That joke really hurt.

If I want you to stop making your jokes, I need to tell you I am hurt by them.

I was getting resistance to the importance of communicating feelings from a group I was training at a software company. People suggested that no one cared how anyone felt. The HR director backed me up by sharing a story. He coached an employee who several managers had found difficult. She was resisting his suggestion that she put people on the defensive— until the HR director said,

I feel defensive talking to you.

That admission opened her eyes to how she impacted others.

Admit what you are feeling to yourself! Then, if you believe it will increase your chances of getting what you want, admit it to the person you are talking to. It's not only healthy—it gets results.

PowerPhrases to Express What You Feel Say What You Mean

Exactly what do you REALLY feel? What do you really mean? Look deeply and communicate the whole story. Are you really angry because your daughter was late coming home? Or are you frightened for her? Or are you angry, frightened, relieved, and frustrated all at once? If so, don't say,

I'm mad at you.

when it would include more of your meaning to say,

I'm so glad you're safe. I was terrified for you. I'm angry with you for scaring me like this and frustrated that this is happening again.

Are you really just upset that your coworker didn't mention your name when she told the boss about your idea? Or are you feeling betrayed? Perhaps you are upset, shocked, and feeling betrayed all at once. Don't say,

I'm upset that you didn't mention my name.

when what you really mean is

It shocked me that you didn't mention my name and I feel betrayed.

When I had a problem with a service provider, I examined what I felt and told her,

While your responses to me have always been professional, I feel scolded for asking what I believe to be a legitimate question. I feel like I'm five years old.

It felt risky to express my feelings to someone who already seemed cold and impersonal. I took the risk—and it worked.

Figure out what is in your heart and choose your words accordingly.

PowerPhrases to Say What You Feel Mean What You Say

Don't express feelings that are a short-term reaction that you will regret later. Mandy was upset with her boss and said,

I don't trust you.

When she calmed down she realized that expression wasn't what she meant. She felt regret and apologized. The damage was done and she wished she had held her tongue. You can never really retract your words.

I have a twenty-four hour rule. If I want to say something when I am emotional and feeling defensive, I promise myself that if I still want to say it in twenty-four hours, I will. Often when the twenty-four hours pass, I realize that I didn't really mean what I thought I did at the time—I was just having a reaction.

So instead of speaking in the moment when your feelings

are jumbled and unclear, tell yourself that if you still mean it in twenty-four hours, you will communicate it.

Whatever you decide to say, be certain that it is genuine. You do not need to express every feeling; in fact, you are better off if you don't. Select the feelings that will work toward your result. In most situations, the most vulnerable feeling you express has the most impact. If you are both angry and concerned, expressing the concern will have the greatest impact.

PowerPhrases to Say What You Feel Are Not Mean When You Say Them

Avoid using feelings as weapons. If someone needs to know how you feel in order to understand you and the situation, express that feeling. If you want to express the feeling to punish them for not giving you what you want, resist the temptation. It will come back to bite you. Don't take them on a guilt trip, and do not use your emotions to intimidate them. Be clear in your intention and resist emotional revenge.

When feelings are an important part of the message, let them know—in clear and direct PowerPhrases.

15

Ask So You Will Receive

PowerPhrases to Make Powerful Requests

Joan was busy, so when Kit mentioned she might ask for help with the new software, she didn't think anything about it. Only later did it occur to Joan that Kit hoped Joan would offer help. Joan would have happily helped if Kit had said,

Will you help me with the new software?

Kit beat around the bush and hinted, and Joan didn't pick up on it.

I understand Kit's hesitation! I used to hate asking for what I want. I was made aware of my woeful, wimpy ways of asking for things thirty years ago when I attempted to hail a taxi in New York City. Many taxis went by. What's up with them? Don't they want my business? When one did stop, the driver told me,

I couldn't tell you wanted a cab. Your signals were not clear.

I'm sure that's not the only time my signals weren't clear! Even hailing a taxi was a frightening experience of putting my needs out there.

I don't know where I got the idea that I wasn't allowed to want or need, but I did. All across the world I encounter people who know exactly what I am talking about when I say this. Getting clear about what you want is the first big step in making powerful requests. Figure out what you really want, and ask for it.

So how do you use PowerPhrases to make powerful requests? The same way you use PowerPhrases to communicate anything. Be brief, specific, and targeted, and say what you mean and mean what you say without being mean when you say it.

PowerPhrases to Make Requests Are Short

Being brief means cutting the fluff! Don't say,

> *I'm sorry to bother you—I mean I know what a busy person you are, but I was hoping that maybe Thursday—well it doesn't have to be Thursday, but Thursday would work for me-and it could be morning and could be the afternoon, it really depends on you. Anyway, I am wondering if you might meet with me just for a few minutes if it's convenient. . . .*

Yuck! Gag! Choke! Do you do this? Do not water your request down with too many words and do not overstate your case with too many words. If you ask,

Will you meet with me for ten minutes on Thursday?

you are more likely to get your results. At least they'll be able to listen long enough to know what you're asking for!

Have you ever had someone ask you for something and you were ready to say "yes" but he was so busy trying to sell you on the idea that you didn't get to tell him? Then, by the time he finally finished and you got to get a PowerPhrase in edgewise, you changed your mind!

Do not be afraid of silence when making requests. Ask and be quiet. Most people hate silence and most people hate saying "no," so if you ask and become silent, your chances for a "yes" are excellent.

PowerPhrases to Make Requests Are Specific

Ask for exactly what you want. If you don't, you may get what you ask for, and not get what you want. A woman in Canada requested a raise, and literally got an additional five cents an hour. She got what she asked for, but not what she wanted.

Sandy was gathering donations for a local charity auction. Everyone was contributing, but the items were small. She remembered about being specific and held her head up high as she went into an office and said,

I am soliciting donations for the Rebuilding America fund-raiser. Will you donate a spa?

They donated a $4,000 spa.

PowerPhrases to Make Requests Are Targeted

You are not making a request for entertainment value—you're asking to get results. You want something they can give you. Ask with this clear question in mind: What do you want and what course of action is likely to get you that result?

When you negotiate with your boss, say for a new copier, what will make it more likely for your boss to say "yes"? Your boss needs to know why it makes sense to him or her for you to have it. That means you don't go in saying,

I need a new copy machine because I hate using the group one.

I'm not saying your boss doesn't care, but he or she probably doesn't care in four figures. You are better off to go in saying,

We have a problem. In the course of a week I spend *w* hours making copies. This is time I could use productively if I had my own machine. While I make *x* dollars per hour, the total cost per hour for the company to employ me is *y*. That means that in the course of a month we spend *z* dollars because I do not have my own copier. However, I've done the research and I have found a machine that will pay for itself by January 1st.

Now you're talking! Now your boss is listening. Now you get results! Learn the ever-popular PowerPhrases,

What this means for you is . . .

This will benefit you by . . .

What can you say that will make the other person *want* to honor your request? In other words, go in thinking of giving, not just getting. You have to regard your request from the other person's perspective. What pressures are on this person? Often, he or she has to sell the deal to other people. Excellent phrases are:

What can I give you that will enable you to get me a better deal?

Would it make a difference if I . . . ?

It's your job to know what is needed and to address that. After all, you are the one who wants something. That means you get to do the work of making your request attractive.

PowerPhrases to Make Requests Say What You Mean

The hallway at my seminar hotel was messy. I mentioned to the banquets manager,

The hallway looks like it hasn't been vacuumed.

He replied, "Oh it has. It's just that when we brought the tables in, it got messy again."

Okay . . . that wasn't the response I was looking for. In my mind I had asked him to vacuum the hallway. Guess what—I didn't really! Do you hear a request in my remark? The ban-quets manager didn't either. Later I asked him,

Will you please vacuum the hallway?

Done. Cheerfully, thoroughly, done. I just had to ask.

Avoid making statements and thinking you are making requests! Avoid saying,

I can hardly make ends meet on this salary.

When what you mean is,

I deserve a 15 percent raise because . . . . Can you do that for me?

Rather than saying,

I wish I had more time for this project.

say,

I need an additional week for this project. How can we make that happen?

And say what you mean with the kids. Replace

The TV is too loud.

with

Turn down the TV now, please.

You have no reason to get upset if you don't get something you never really asked for. Say what you mean. If you want something, ask! Clearly, directly, ask!

PowerPhrases to Make Requests Mean What You Say

If you need a raise to stay with the company, explain that when you request your raise. If you know leaving is not an option for you, don't mention it. Only mention it if you mean it.

If you need an assistant to meet a deadline, say so. If you are saying that simply because you prefer help even though you don't really need it, leave it out. And if you offer anything in exchange for what you want be certain you follow through.

The PowerPhrase to communicate your intended course of action is

I will . . .

PowerPhrases Requests Are Not Mean When You Say Them

Julie and Jennifer were standing around the reception desk complaining about one of the directors in the company. Julie said, "She never asks us to do things. She just drops it on the desk and says, 'Here—do this.' Well, I'm not going to do it. I'm just going to tell her I couldn't get to it. And the next time she gets a fax, I'm not dropping everything to bring it to her." Jennifer replied, "I wouldn't drop everything for her if she was drowning."

I left out a few of the adjectives they used.

Many people who always bend over backwards for those who treat them with respect won't even budge for someone who doesn't.

Be certain to consider the listener when you make requests.

Give me this or else.

This style may work short-term. It won't work in the long-run.

Phrase your request in the positive rather than the negative. Avoid

Don't make mistakes.

because it sounds friendlier to say,

This needs to be error-free.

Rather than saying,

Don't come after 3:00 P.M.

say,

Come before 3:00 P.M.

Rather than saying,

Please don't send so many e-mails.

say,

Please consolidate your e-mails into one or two each day.

Eliminate sarcasm. Forget requests like,

I don't suppose you could pick up the phone and call, could you?

Sarcasm is the low road. PowerPhrases are the high road. Power-Phrases are what will get you what you want when it's all said and done.

16

The Power of Saying NO!

PowerPhrases to Refuse What You Don't Want

It was an honor to be invited to join the conference's featured speaker for dinner and Deb gladly went. She wasn't hungry, so she just went along for the company. Deb had a baked potato. The others enjoyed a several-course meal. The wine and champagne flowed freely. At the end of the meal, the group decided to split the bill. Deb's baked potato cost her $70!

The next day Deb complained to everyone about how unfair it was—yet her real issue was with herself. She was the one who went along with the decision rather than to say "no."

Robert, in a similar situation, told the group,

I'm not comfortable splitting the bill because I didn't eat much. I am very happy to pay my portion and a little extra. I'm comfortable with $20.

Yes, it was awkward for the group for a moment, but had Robert paid the divided tab he would have felt used and resentful. Then a wealthy woman said, "No problem. I'll pay for everyone!" That improved everyone's moods!

Using PowerPhrases to say "no" is so simple, so straightforward, and so powerful! It doesn't make anyone wrong; it simply expresses your perspective.

That doesn't mean it's easy. According to my informal surveys about two out of three of us have a "No-Saying-Deficiency." Read on for the road to recovery.

PowerPhrases to Say "No" Are Short

Well, for most cases "just say no" is a bit too short. But forget the long explanations that sound like excuses! You don't have to go into a detailed explanation.

Recently, I asked a friend named Dawn if she could cover a speaking engagement for me. She said,

Thanks for thinking of me, but I'm not available that day. Ask again sometime.

Okay, Dawn, I'm waiting! I'm waiting for you to explain why. What could you possibly be doing that is more important than helping me out here? C'mon, and it better be good!

No explanation followed.

It felt odd. It felt incomplete. It felt . . . healthy! Why should she have to explain why she couldn't cover for me? I was expecting her to explain simply because most people do. I respect the fact that she didn't.

An effective "no" is limited to three sentences.

Begin with an **Acknowledgment** such as,

> I see this is important.

> I would if I could.

> What a great idea!

Follow with brief **Clarification** of your situation,

> I have other priorities.

> I'm already committed.

> I'm not comfortable with that.

Finally conclude with a **Tag phrase** to reinforce the relationship.

> Thanks for asking.

> Perhaps next time.

> I hope you find someone who can help you.

That's it! No more! Take inspiration from my friend Dawn and forget the wordiness.

PowerPhrases to Say "No" Are Specific

Understand, when I tell you to be specific, I'm not talking a lot of detail here. Just be certain that it is clear what you are saying "no" to. Robert said "no" to splitting the bill, but he did not say "no" to paying anything. He was specific when he said,

I'm comfortable paying $20.

Dawn wasn't saying "no" to ever covering a speaking engagement for me. She was saying "no" to that day. She said,

Ask again sometime.

Perhaps you are saying "no" to part of a request. Be specific. If someone is taking a collection and you don't want to contribute the recommended amount, say,

I'd love to chip in $2 to the collection. Five dollars is more than I am willing to pitch in.

I'll cover for you for fifteen minutes while you find someone else who can cover the rest of the day.

Being specific means being clear. It does NOT mean going into detailed excuses and explanations.

PowerPhrases to Say "No" Are Targeted

"No" is one of the biggest time-saving devices in existence. Figure out exactly what you want before you speak. If you want to avoid being asked again, choose words that will accomplish that. Rather than,

Not this time.

say,

> **Thanks for asking, but it's not something that interests me.**

If you want to stay on their list, choose words that will encourage them to ask again. Say,

> **I wish I could, but if you try again another time I might be able to. Keep asking, will you?**

If you want to increase rapport while drawing a boundary, choose words that reinforce the relationship. Know what matters most and target words that will accomplish that.

PowerPhrases to Say "No"; Say What You Mean

When John asked Chandra to do some lettering for him, she replied,

> *Someone else would be better suited to do the lettering. I'm not good at it. I don't think you want me to do this.*

Is that what Chandra really meant? John wasn't sure. John believed Chandra was well-suited to help, so he started to explain why he wanted her to do it. He was building her up. He was telling her how talented she was. He was supporting her.

The problem was that Chandra wasn't saying what she meant. So John's conversation was way off track. Chandra knew she was good. She just didn't want to do it.

Chandra and John both would have been better off if Chandra had said,

I know I'm good at lettering, but I don't enjoy it. Thanks for asking, but I don't want to.

Hannah told her sister Ellen,

Now isn't the best time to visit. I won't be able to give you the attention you need.

Ellen didn't need attention. She just wanted to hang around. She already had her tickets. She had scheduled her vacation. But the issue wasn't really about whether Hannah could give Ellen attention or not. The issue was that Hannah had been seriously overworked and needed downtime. Ellen would have understood had Hannah said,

I'd love to see you, but I'm overworked and am desperate for downtime. I am so sorry to have to back out on this visit, but I need to.

Forget the hints and say what you mean. When you only hint, you put pressure on the other person to decipher your meaning.

PowerPhrases to Say "No"; Mean What You Say

Meaning what you say is the hardest part about saying "no." Before you speak, be sure you will back yourself up.

A 2002 survey by the Center for a New American Dream confirms how often "no" means "maybe." According to the survey, the average American child aged 12 to 17 will ask nine times for what he or she wants before the parents will give in. More than 12 percent of thirteen-year-olds admit to asking parents for what they want fifty times or more.

Why? Because it works. They've learned when their parents do not mean their "no"s.

Do yourself a favor and ask yourself: Do you intend to back your words up with action? Do you mean your "no"? If you don't, then don't even say it. Say "no" only if you mean it.

PowerPhrases to Say "No" Are Not Mean When You Say Them

Please be aware that many people are uncomfortable asking for things. Avoid making them regret asking. Avoid saying,

No (unless he is the kind of person who requires that kind of directness).

Why would I want to do that?

You're kidding, right?

No way.

Often when people are asked to do something they don't want to do, they feel guilty for saying "no." However, they often communicate anger instead of guilt. People have a right to ask, and you have a right to say "no." It's interesting that often the more free you feel to say "no," the more free they can feel to ask. When you do say "no," include a brief statement that acknowledges them and the relationship. Honor them while you stand firm with what you want.

17

Listen So They Speak Freely

PowerPhrases to Get Them to Open Up

It was one of those meetings from you know where. Sheila was on the warpath. Nothing we said was getting through. Everything we said was a threat to her. Everything we said was an attack on her. This 6'2", 195-pound woman was acting as if she was the innocent victim of everyone and everything. Nothing helped, until someone said,

Let's do active listening with Sheila. Let's allow her to talk until she feels completely heard.

Sheila liked that idea! She talked and we listened. I don't recall her saying anything memorable. I just remember that her defenses dropped and she became human again. Once we listened with our undivided attention, it took all of about three minutes for Sheila to relax, to get off her defenses, and to be open again to what we said. You give a gift when you practice listening. That's why you need PowerPhrases for listening!

It was a special day for Bob and me. We went for the same walk we take every week. We watched the same shows, ate the same food, and did the same things. Something was special. What was it?

When the day ended, Bob asked, "Did you enjoy being with me today?" "Very much," I responded. He explained, "Today, I decided I was going to listen to you all day and put myself on hold." I had no idea! I just thought we were getting along great.

You give a gift when you practice listening. That's why you need PowerPhrases for listening!

Yep! PowerPhrases to open them up, to draw them out, to keep them talking. You need PowerPhrases that are short, specific, targeted, and say what you mean, and mean what you say, without being mean when you say them.

PowerPhrases for Listening Are Short

If you're talking, you're not listening! So while you will want to make short statements to encourage them to talk, your comments need to be brief enough to allow them all the room they need to talk. The speaker will appreciate short PowerPhrases like:

Tell me more.

I hear you.

What else?

The speakers will not appreciate any attempts to sneak your own agenda in or your long-winded comments that derail them from saying what they need to.

PowerPhrases for Listening Are Specific

"You're not listening to me!" William exclaimed.

Yes I am!

his boss, Sue, defended. Maybe she was. If she was, it wasn't helping. William wasn't feeling heard. When Sue changed what she said to

What I hear you saying is . . .

William calmed.

You need to choose words that assure your listeners that they have been heard. Those words must be carefully selected to specifically reflect what they are saying to you. When William's boss told him what she heard him say, he felt heard. When Sheila heard us repeat back what she said at the meeting, she felt heard. Your responses will not be the same for everyone in every situation. Your responses need to be specific to reflect what they are telling you.

PowerPhrases for Listening Are Targeted

Consciously choose goals before you begin to listen. Effective listening goals are to (A) make them feel safe, (B) draw them out, (C) understand them, and (D) ensure that they feel heard, understood and honored.

A) PowerPhrases That Make Them Feel Safe

Sheila responded to our efforts because she felt safe. Once she knew that she could say anything, she wanted without any argument, her defenses dropped. PowerPhrases to help that happen are:

I want to hear what you have to say.

I didn't know you felt that way.

I see why that would be an issue for you.

I can imagine how that might have felt.

I appreciate you being so open with me.

B) PowerPhrases That Draw Them Out

Bob drew me out on our magical day by making the day about me. He put himself on hold. If he did that forever, I wouldn't feel safe, but with the foundation of safety that we have with each other, it was delightful. PowerPhrases that aid this process are:

Tell me more.

What else can you tell me about that?

That's an interesting point.

What did you like about that?

C) PowerPhrases to Ensure That You Understand

Be very careful asking clarifying questions when your goal is to listen. Be sure that your own agenda doesn't slip in with the questions. All clarifying questions need to be aimed at eliminating any confusion about what the speaker is telling you. PowerPhrases that aid this process are:

Help me to understand.

I'm a bit confused about . . .

What were you referring to when you said . . . ?

I didn't catch something you said a minute ago.

D) PowerPhrases That Make Them Feel Heard, Understood, and Honored

All of the listening phrases will add to the speaker's feeling of being heard. Some specific PowerPhrases for this process are:

Let me make sure I understand what you are saying. I believe you are saying . . .

So when _____ happened you felt _____?

What you need from me is . . . . Am I right?

Whenever you are in a crucial conversation and the other person seems to need to express her thoughts, feelings, and wants, slip into listening mode and pick PowerPhrases that will get you where you want to go. You cannot get someone to listen who needs to be heard herself.

PowerPhrase for Listening Say What You Mean

Listening is not about you, so you won't want to take the focus off them. Just be certain to be sincere in your listening phrases.

Why do you want to listen to them? Express the reason in your heart for wanting to listen. Say,

I want to be certain I know what it's like for you.

I believe you are a reasonable person and I want to understand the reasoning that went into that decision.

I value our relationship, and I don't want any kind of misunderstanding to interfere with it. I want to understand you as much as possible.

If you are only listening because you know it's the only way you can get them to listen to you, you probably won't want to share that part of what you mean. But why do you care in the first place? Is it because you value their opinion of you? Is it because you know they carry a lot of weight in the department? Somewhere in your heart and mind, there is a thought, a feeling, and a desire that will build a bridge if you express it.

PowerPhrases for Listening Mean What You Say

Avoid telling them,

I want to hear what you have to say.

and then arguing with them when they try to tell you.
Avoid saying,

You can talk to me.

and proceed to make them wish they hadn't tried.
Steer clear of saying,

Help me to understand.

and proceed to stop listening as soon as they say the first thing you don't agree with. This is a delicate process. Keep the integrity of your words. Mean what you say.

PowerPhrases for Listening Are Not Mean When You Say Them

Listening is about creating safety. At the first sign of judgment, blame, accusation, or rejection, your friend, family member, boss, or coworker is likely to clam up. Listen with your heart open.

Avoid saying,

You don't mean that.

I don't believe you.

That's ridiculous.

You can express your perspective later, and when you do, be certain to do it in a way that does not make them regret opening up to you.

Whether you believe there is validity in what they are saying or not, once you invite people to open up, it is important to honor their words. Yes, you can disagree, but you must honor their trust in talking by respecting them and their words.

18

When You Really Blew It

PowerPhrases to Apologize Sincerely without Groveling

Recently a man named Tony Graves was sentenced to life in prison in Fort Collins, Colorado, for a string of assaults. At the hearing, many of his victims and their families expressed their anger in words filled with venom. They were very specific about the horrors they hoped Tony would experience in prison. I was struck by Tony's response. He said:

> The past is unchangeable. If it makes anyone feel better, all the things the victims wish for me will probably come true. All the anger and hate, I understand that. Give it all to me. But don't let it affect you.

If there were any right words for a time like that, those were the words. Understandably, however, the victims were unimpressed.

Stephen Covey's words in *The 7 Habits of Highly Effective People* apply here. He said,

You cannot talk your way out of something you acted your way into.

It will take a lifetime for Tony to gain forgiveness.

I assume your mistakes are more trivial. Whatever mistakes you are apologizing for, it is important that you apologize with PowerPhrase grace.

While you can't talk your way out of something you acted your way into, you can smooth some feathers by using short, specific, targeted expressions to say what you mean and mean what you say without being mean when you say them.

PowerPhrases to Apologize Sincerely without Groveling Are Short

Keep your apology to a few sentences. Groveling happens when you keep going after it has all been said. Don't plead, beg, or whine. Just apologize. When you go on too long, everyone gets uncomfortable.

PowerPhrases to Apologize Sincerely without Groveling Are Specific

A generic

I'm sorry.

is too vague to be effective. Explain specifically why you regret what you did. Say,

> **You were counting on me and I let you down.**

> **I care about you and what I did doesn't honor that.**

> **I hate to see you hurting and hate it even more to know I caused it.**

Ask yourself: Why are you sorry? What can you acknowledge in their experience that will make them feel heard and understood? You need to address the pain or inconvenience you caused them to be effective. Be specific to what happened. If you are apologizing for losing an application, acknowledge the specific inconvenience and hardship they experienced as a result. If you are apologizing for missing an appointment, apologize for the impact that had.

PowerPhrases to Apologize Sincerely without Groveling Are Targeted

Why do you want to apologize? If forgiveness is the result you seek, or at least some mending of the relationship, keep that goal firmly in mind. That means avoid saying,

> *You know, I'm not the only one who messed up here.*

or making excuses. Accept full responsibility for your role in what happened and don't worry about their role. That's another discussion that you may or may not choose to have later.

Some things can't be forgiven, but the chances that your apology will be accepted are greater when you apologize effectively.

I like Tony's words so much because they were spoken without defensiveness or excuses. Tony made no attempt to justify or blame. Tony accepted the wrongness of his actions and the appropriateness of the judgments that were made about him. He spoke to the perspective and to the need of his victims without judgment of them. His crimes may be far too heinous to be forgiven for a high-minded moment. Yet I was impressed that Tony had that moment in him. If you want results, take a lesson from Tony. Avoid the temptation to defend or share blame when you apologize.

PowerPhrases to Apologize Sincerely without Groveling Say What You Mean

Do not apologize if you don't mean it. Ask yourself what you think, feel, and want. Balance those considerations with the results you seek. Maybe you think you blew it, but they are overreacting. If you want the apology to be effective, let them have their outrage and give them time to calm down. Find your meaning that is in line with your communication goals. Then say,

I'm sorry.

I know I . . .

Please forgive me.

If you really blew it, add,

I want to make it up to you. How can I do that?

While you cannot talk your way out of something you acted your way into, a sincere admission of what you mean with promise of restitution and better behavior often helps.

PowerPhrases to Apologize Sincerely without Groveling Mean What You Say

An insincere apology is worse than no apology at all. If you say you are sorry but continue the offending behavior, your actions contradict your words. Apologize only if you mean it. Resist the temptation to say,

I'm sorry to have to tell you—you're an idiot.

Only promise things you believe you can follow up on. Do not agree to make it up somehow and then not follow through. You need to show your regret by action. If they ask for some form of restitution, you cannot agree to, say,

I do sincerely regret what I did. And I need to be realistic in what I agree to. I do not want to let you down again. Let's find some other way for me to make it up to you that I am certain I can agree to.

PowerPhrases to Apologize Sincerely without Groveling Are Not Being Mean When You Apologize

What if you were in their shoes? How would you feel? What would you need? Speak from your heart with the understanding that the other person has been harmed and has every right to be upset. Don't compound your error by faulting others for their reaction.

19

To Get Good Answers You Need Good Questions

Asking Questions with PowerPhrases

Have you ever had one of those days where you longed to go back to bed almost as soon as you got out of it? If you have, you can understand my day in Reno. I was presenting a seminar to a group of eighty women, and the program manager did not show up. I had to do the entire set-up and registration on my own in addition to leading the presentation. I started a few minutes late and was a bit distracted.

I never want to start a seminar with an apology, so I began with a question instead. I asked,

How many of you ever had a day when someone didn't show up and you found yourself doing your job and their job too? (Hands shot up.) **I am having one of those days today.**

Pat yourself on the back, Meryl—that was brilliant! (I love it when my stories make me look good!) Let me tell you why it was brilliant. Had I just said,

> *My program manager didn't show up today, and I'm on my own.*

people would have thought I was complaining. By tying it into an experience they have all had, they remembered a similar experience of their own and felt connected to me. By making the remark in the form of a question, I forced them to ask themselves about their own experience, and they immediately got more involved. That is the value of questions. They get people involved.

My intention was to get you involved by starting this chapter with a question. My objective was to draw you in so you feel like we are taking this journey together.

I ask you questions throughout this book, and you need to ask others questions throughout your day. Skillful questions create a bond. Use PowerPhrases to ask questions—short, specific, targeted expressions to say what you mean and mean what you say without being mean when you say them.

PowerPhrase Questions Are Short

I do several media interviews every week, and I notice that skilled interviewers often use the PowerPhrase Principles for their questions.

Occasionally a deejay or anchor will ask me questions that are so complex that I will forget the question before I can answer. I also get multiple questions tied together. Recently an interviewer asked me, "Tell me about using PowerPhrases for managing bosses, managing coworkers, managing employees, and what unique issues there are in each." When the question is too long, the listener can lose the point. Keep the questions brief and ask one at a time.

PowerPhrase Questions Are Specific

I'm used to it now, but the first time an interviewer opened with the question, "What can you tell me about PowerPhrases," I stumbled. Where do I start? Now I start by saying whatever I want to say (YES!), but until I figured that out, the question seemed too vague to get a grip on.

Asking a job applicant,

Tell me about yourself.

won't get you the same amount of information as asking,

Tell me about your most valuable skill.

That said, be wary of asking questions that are so specific as to "lead the witness." If you are a manager and you need to investigate whether Joe sexually harassed Frieda, instead of asking,

Did you hear Joe tell Frieda that he would give her his stats in exchange for a kiss?

ask,

What did you hear Joe say to Frieda about the reports?

Ask yourself: Will your question get you the specific information you are looking for?

PowerPhrase Questions Are Targeted

There are many objectives for asking questions: 1) to get the listener involved (most of my questions in this book are to get you thinking and involved), 2) to find out what someone knows, 3) to see whether someone means what he or she is saying, 4) to make sure you were clear, 5) to gather information, 6) to regain the balance of control in a conversation.

To get people thinking and involved, use PowerPhrase questions like,

Have you ever had the experience . . . ?

What do you do when . . . ?

Wouldn't you like to . . . ?

Can you imagine . . . ?

To find out what someone knows ask,

How do you do this process?

What is your understanding of . . . ?

What do you know about . . . ?

To learn if someone means what he or she says, ask,

What I heard you say was . . . . Did I hear you correctly?

Let me make certain I understand you correctly. My understanding is . . .

Are you committing to . . . ?

Are you saying that . . . ?

Also, ask questions that get participants to say what they are committing to rather than agreeing to something you have said. Instead of asking,

Will I have the report by Tuesday?

ask,

When are you committing to get that report to me?

You can be more certain of their commitment when you hear the words come out of their mouths.

To see if you were clear in your explanations, rather than asking,

Do you understand?

Do you have questions?

Do you get it?

you will get better results if you focus your questions on your explanations rather than on their understanding,

Let me make sure my instructions were clear. What is your understanding of what I am saying?

What questions remain?

What else would you like to know?

With PowerPhrases you take responsibility for the communication and imply that if they don't get it, it's because you haven't explained it well. People are afraid to look stupid and will hesitate to ask questions if they think it implies that they are.

To clarify your understanding of what they are saying, say,

What I heard you say was . . . is that correct?

Let me make certain I understand you correctly. My understanding is . . . is that accurate?

My impression of your situation is . . . . Am I right?

As I heard you say . . .

To gather information, PowerPhrase questions are,

I'm interested in learning about . . .

Let me ask you this . . .

Help me understand . . .

Could you help me with . . . ?

Could you expand on that for me . . . ?

These are open-ended questions. That means they require more than a one-word answer. When you ask

Can you tell me anything about . . . ?

Do you . . . ?

Would it work to . . . ?

you are using a closed-ended question that will provide less information.

Finally, it's important to know how to use questions to regain balance of control in a conversation. I thought I was in an inquisition one day in an interview to tailor training for a corporation. The HR director fired question after question at me, and I did not feel myself to be in a position of power. At one point she asked, "How would you handle the information on organizing the day?" I responded with a question of my own,

How would you like for me to handle it?

It was a subtle shift, but I felt I was an equal in the conversation from then on, because I had broken the pattern.

Remember this approach the next time someone gets you

in a corner with questions. PowerPhrase questions to regain control of a conversation are:

Why do you ask that?

Are you asking me if . . . ?

What specifically do you want to know about . . . ?

How would YOU respond to that question?

Pick your goal—then pick your PowerPhrases.

PowerPhrase Questions Say What You Mean

How do you say something you DON'T mean with questions? Is there such a thing as an insincere question?

You can ask questions you don't want answers to. You can ask questions so they think you are interested in them, when you are only interested in you. You can ask questions to make them jump through hoops. You can ask questions that attempt to get someone else to say something so you don't have to.

If your questions have a self-serving hidden agenda and if you are being manipulative, you are not saying what you mean. To manipulate means "to play upon or control by artful, unfair, or insidious means." (Remember that definition. Next time someone backs you into corner say, "Hey—You're playing upon me by artful, unfair, or insidious means!")

The key part of the definition is in the word "insidious." Many skillful communicators say things for undisclosed pur-

poses. Before I posed my first question to you, I didn't say—
"I'm going to make this point in the form of a question, so you
will start thinking and get involved." I wasn't being manipulative. There was nothing insidious in my intent.

If you ask questions to trick someone, to gain an unfair
advantage, or to twist the truth, you are not using PowerPhrases.

PowerPhrase Questions Mean What You Say

Have you ever asked someone if he wanted something, feeling
confident he would refuse? You got points for asking, but
didn't have to do something you did not care to do. Conve-
nient, perhaps, but manipulative. Be sure you mean what your
questions imply you mean.

PowerPhrase Questions Are Not Mean When You Say Them

PowerPhrases are tools—not weapons. Questions can be either.
The following examples are weapons:

How long have you been beating your wife?

Are you always this stupid?

What, I look like an idiot?

These are set-up questions that are intended manipulatively and
are not PowerPhrases.

Watch out for interrogation. Firing question after question without any self-disclosure is an intimidation tactic and not a PowerPhrase.

While asking questions to balance an out-of-balance conversation is appropriate, asking questions to control a conversation is inappropriate. Sales professionals know they can control an entire conversation with questions. The sales profession is developing into a service profession and the industry has woken up to the fact that manipulation can work in the short-run but doesn't build relationships in the long-run. PowerPhrases are about long-term effectiveness.

20

You Don't Have to Put Up with Put-Downs

PowerPhrase Responses to Unkind Criticism

Emily found a job she really wanted in a doctor's office. It didn't last very long. Her boss was very unkind in his words. I call the doctor "Dr. Awful."

Dr. Awful would say things like,

What kind of idiot are you?

Can't you follow any directions?

My dog can do a better job than you can.

For two weeks, Emily endured his comments and for two weeks her self-esteem plummeted. Finally, she couldn't take it anymore. She picked up her purse and walked out.

We found out about the person who had the job after her. Marie loved her job—and she loved her boss! She taught him how to treat her early on. When Dr. Awful asked,

What kind of idiot are you?

Marie didn't suffer in silence. She also didn't say,

The same kind of idiot as the person who hired me.

She said,

When you ask, "What kind of idiot are you," I get confused and actually make more mistakes. I need for you to give me support when I make mistakes.

When Dr. Awful said,

Can't you follow any directions?

Marie didn't doubt her ability to follow directions. She also didn't say,

I could if they weren't given by a moron.

She said,

I find your directions difficult to follow. Let's sit down and find a way for you to give directions that I find easier to follow.

When Dr. Awful said,

My dog can do a better job than you can.

Marie didn't take the insult in. She also didn't say,

Hire your dog!

She said,

**I find that remark very insulting. I am a professional
and I do expect to be treated as one.**

Marie taught Dr. Awful how to treat her from the very first day
and he listened.

Some people hear this story and wonder why Marie bothered. They say, "Someone who speaks that way doesn't deserve
respect and isn't worth the trouble."

They may be right—but sometimes you will have a situation
where it is worth your trouble to handle the Dr. Awfuls in your
life. You need to know how.

This was a big issue for me, because I grew up with a lot of
sarcasm and put-downs. I don't have those in my life anymore.
Like Marie, I have rooted them out.

People give unkind criticism for three reasons: (1) they are
just plain mean and they have been getting away with it, (2)
they have a real concern and don't know how to address the
issue directly, and (3) it is a habit they are unaware of. Whatever reason, the cure is the same: PowerPhrases!

PowerPhrase Responses to Put-Downs Are Short

Your best comeback is one to three sentences. Any more gives
the attacker ammunition for a rejoinder and sounds defensive.
PowerPhrases are as long as they need to be and no longer.

PowerPhrase Responses to Put-Downs Are Specific

Tell attackers exactly how their words affected you and how you want to be treated instead. Don't say,

Stop that!

say,

> **That remark hurts because I care about your opinion and it sounds like you are trying to discourage me. If you have an issue, let's discuss it directly.**

> **I worked very hard to make this party a success. If I have not met your expectations, tell me what's wrong, but don't take potshots.**

Ask yourself—exactly what in their words was hurtful? Why was it hurtful? How do you want to be treated? Be specific.

PowerPhrase Responses to Unkind Criticism Are Targeted

Your goal is to stop attackers in their tracks. Your goal is to put an end to the digs.

When someone gives you an unkind put-down, he is being passive-aggressive. Your response needs to be assertive. That puts an end to it, regardless of the motivation.

If they attack you out of meanness, when you are assertive they will stop. It's no fun for them if you don't let it get to you.

If they are used to getting away with hit and run tactics,

when you are assertive they soon discover they can't get away with it and they stop.

If they are laying it on you because they have an issue and don't know how to communicate any other way, an invitation to speak openly will eliminate their attack.

If it is a habit they are unaware of, telling them makes them aware.

Target your words toward the result you want.

PowerPhrase Responses to Unkind Criticism Say What You Mean

Tell the truth about what you think, feel, and want.

I think that remark was hurtful and uncalled for.

I feel disappointed and affronted.

I want to be treated with respect.

Or,

I think there must be something else bothering you for you to make a remark like that.

I feel offended.

I want to discuss anything that may be creating tension between us.

Or,

That remark sounded like a dig.

I am insulted.

I expect to be treated with respect.

I don't understand why you would speak that way.

Your response to their words gives you the meaning you need to communicate in your PowerPhrases.

PowerPhrase Responses to Put-Downs Mean What You Say

I was on an airplane sitting next to a man and woman. The man was taking potshots at the woman every chance he got. When we got up to leave, I asked if they were married, hoping for her sake that they weren't! He replied,

Yes—I married this.

She said an ineffective

Oh, stop!

It was clear that she didn't expect him to change a thing in response to her words. She was swatting flies.

When someone puts you down, don't speak as a test to see if he will comply. You are not throwing words out hoping he will pick up on it. PowerPhrases will only end unkind criticism when you really intend to end it.

It does not work to stand up to the side-swipes once and ignore them another time. Stay committed to insisting that you want to be treated with respect. If you tell them you won't be spoken to that way, and then take it when they speak that way again, you invite more abuse. Also, avoid telling them you want to address issues directly and then make it hard for them to be honest with you. Mean what you say.

What would I have had that woman tell her husband? How could she have responded with firmness and dignity? How about,

I do not deserve that remark and you know it.

That remark is inappropriate and uncalled for.

PowerPhrase Responses to Put-Downs Are Not Mean When You Say Them

It is important to SpeakStrong when someone puts you down, and it is important that you don't stoop to her level of Vicious Venom Poison Phrases.

I would not have advised my airplane seatmate to take a shot back at her depreciating husband. I would not have advised her to say,

A loser like you is lucky to have me!

It takes a lot of courage to take the high road when someone is being unkind to you. That's the only way to break the cycle. Be willing to do what works, and do what will turn them around. Be clear about your intention to be respected and kind in your way of insisting. Avoid trying to match them or out-clever them. No getting back at them, no counter-attacks. Someone needs to remain the adult, and I want it to be you! Stay assertive—say what you mean and mean what you say, without being mean when you say it.

21

Don't Resist Anger, Defuse It

PowerPhrases to Handle the Angry Person

When you dissolve a partnership of any kind, whether it's a business partnership or a marriage, it can be an ugly breeding ground for hurt feelings and anger. When Carmen and her partner, Mickey, were discussing the terms for dissolving their partnership, Mickey would become angry, Carmen would react, and they never got closer to a resolution. Then one day Carmen had dental work done. To help with the pain, she was given painkillers.

When the subject of how to divide things came up, Mickey attacked as usual. Carmen did not react. For about an hour Mickey hurled angry insults and attacks at Carmen. Carmen was feeling no pain. She listened, acknowledged, and did not react. Instead, she said things like,

I can understand that.

I can see why you would see it that way.

You have put a lot of energy into this business.

You're right, you do work hard.

All her phrases were chosen to acknowledge Mickey's perspective without invalidating her own.

After a full hour, Mickey calmed down. Carmen saw the opportunity to present her proposal. She asked,

Are you open to hearing my ideas of how we can divide things up?

Mickey replied, "Yeah, I suppose." Carmen calmly presented her plan (which had been carefully crafted to reflect his thinking and needs in the situation as well as her own). She was stunned when Mickey said, "That sounds acceptable."

Carmen found the answer to dealing with Mickey's anger—and it wasn't painkillers! She learned the power of not resisting anger, but defusing it instead.

Carmen had discovered that her previous responses to Mickey had only fueled his anger. Carmen also discovered that when she did not react to Mickey, he calmed down. Carmen realized she had the power to defuse his anger if she could find the power in herself to resist making counter-attacks.

There is great power in non-resistance. Gandhi knew it. Martin Luther King, Jr. knew it. I bet you know it too, and forget when the heat is on. It pays to remember.

PowerPhrases to Handle the Angry Person Are Short

When someone is angry, let him talk. Say only enough to show that you are listening. Use PowerPhrases for listening. Defusing anger is as much about what you don't say as what you do. Someone who is venting anger needs to talk. That means you keep quiet so he can talk. **Carmen had the most successful communication of her partnership the day she said the least.** When Mickey had his say without resistance, he became open to her.

PowerPhrases to Handle the Angry Person Are Specific

Be attentive to exactly what the angry person says. This person wants to be understood for the exact reasons that caused the anger. If your coworker is angry because no one told her that the shipment would be delayed, rather than saying,

I'm sorry the shipment was delayed.

acknowledge the real reason she is upset: No one told her. Make your comments specific. Say,

I'm sorry no one told you about the delay.

If your boss is upset because you didn't apologize for an error, don't say,

I know that error is upsetting to you.

The error may be the issue for you, but if it was the apology that got her bent into a pretzel, say,

Accountability is important to you, and by not apologizing I can see that I was not accountable.

Let your words be specific to their needs.

PowerPhrases to Handle an Angry Person Are Targeted

Sometimes people accuse me of contradicting myself. I say you don't have to put up with put-downs. Then I say when someone is venting anger you need to put your reactions on hold while she hurls accusations at you in a not-so-gracious way. What's real?

PowerPhrases are purposeful. When someone is angry, she is not open to hearing you. When someone is angry, your first step is to defuse the anger and to calm the person down. That usually means you need to listen first and acknowledge the anger. It occasionally means to stand up to her about how she is speaking, but it never means arguing with her.

People are the least loveable when they need love the most. An angry person often needs love, acceptance, or at least acknowledgement to be open to hearing what you have to say.

Do what works. Say,

I want to resolve this because I like working with you and don't want anything to upset that.

I'm sorry this misunderstanding happened because I care about our relationship.

I value your account and take your concerns to heart.

It can be difficult, because if someone is venting anger, the challenge is to remember that this situation simply involves a good person who is upset.

Some people vent in order to intimidate you into giving them what they want. In this case, you still want to stay calm. But if listening doesn't calm them, you will need to be firm. You can say,

I understand you're upset and your anger will not get me to change my policy.

If I could give you what you are asking for I would do it without your anger. I'm not able and your anger will not change that.

Whatever approach you take, do not give them a fight. It is difficult to win a fight with an angry person.

You must stay calm yourself. Stay calm—but not computer-like. Calm compassion and concern soothes the raging beast in all of us.

PowerPhrases to Handle the Angry Person Say What You Mean

Saying what you mean doesn't imply that you have to say EVERYTHING you mean. If you think they are an idiot, don't tell them. If you think they are a narcissistic fool, don't tell them. You may mean it, but that's not enough! Find something you mean that will lead you toward your goal.

Are you frightened when people get angry? Sometimes that will add power by bringing up the humanness of the angry person. Try saying,

I am frightened by your anger.

if you believe they will respond to vulnerability. If you believe they won't respect that, leave it out. If you are not frightened by anger, you might want to let them know that. Say,

I'm not frightened by your anger.

Do you have trouble hearing the issues when someone is angry? An excellent PowerPhrase is

I want to focus on the issues but I find the intensity of your words distracting.

Remember, when someone is angry, your reactive self will find meaning that will have no relevance once you've calmed. When you say what you mean, say what you mean in the bigger sense, looking beyond the current emotional situation. It takes a lot of discipline when someone is angry to ask yourself what is underneath your reaction to his behavior. The road to resolution will be contained in the deeper meaning.

PowerPhrases to Handle the Angry Person Mean What You Say

Do not let angry people bully you into promising something you can't deliver. You may be tempted to say whatever they want to hear. You set yourself up if you do.

Avoid saying,

I'll get you a refund.

if you're not sure you can.
Avoid saying,

This will never happen again.

if you can't guarantee it.
Avoid saying,

I'm not listening to this.

and then proceed to listen.
Be sure you mean every word you say.

PowerPhrases to Handle the Angry Person Are Not Mean When You Say Them

I don't care how inappropriate the angry person is. Your job is to stay full of integrity. No matter how passive, aggressive, or passive-aggressive they are, you need to take the high road. It's the right thing to do—and it works.

Listen and speak with compassion and an eye on your chosen goal. Avoid blame, attack, and resistance.

Be careful about your choice of words to avoid inviting misinterpretation. Avoid saying,

You shouldn't be angry.

when what you really mean is,

It was not my intention to offend you.

If you tell them they shouldn't be angry, they will only hear judgment of their anger not of your intended message of good-will.

Avoid saying,

I'm sorry you misunderstood me.

when they need to hear

I'm sorry I wasn't clear.

Otherwise, they will hear blame and accusation.

Never, ever, use sarcasm with angry people. Keep your heart open to them and their need in their anger.

The next time someone is angry with you, don't resist. Defuse his or her anger with PowerPhrases.

22

Use Anger as a Tool, Not as a Weapon

PowerPhrases to Express Anger

There is nothing wrong with anger. Anger is a message that you feel violated in some way. Anger is a signal that something needs to change. Respect your anger. That does not mean doing whatever your anger dictates. You do not want your anger to control you. You want to work *with* your anger to get results.

Sandy did not have that awareness. Sandy was a fight waiting to happen at the airport one day. When Sandy arrived at the check-in counter, she looked at the monitor and noticed an earlier flight home. She scurried to see if she could catch it.

When she reached security, she quickly put her bag on the belt. As she walked through the X-ray, she heard the dreaded beep-beep-beep. No problem—Sandy knew it was her shoes, and she knew what to do.

She went to secondary screening and handed her shoes to

be cleared as the security personnel wanded her. When the wand passed over her torso, once again she heard the dreaded beep-beep-beep. The underwire in her bra had triggered the wand, so the female security personnel started to pat Sandy down. Sandy was extremely uncomfortable with the process and said in scathing words,

You don't need to do that. It's the f—— underwire of my bra.

The lady said, "Ma'am, you need to calm down. I do need to do this." Sandy barked,

This is NOT REALLY NECESSARY! It's the f—— UNDERWIRE in my bra. You're treating me like a common criminal.

The security woman called over another security guard, "I need some help here. We have a hostile passenger." The guard asked Sandy, "What seems to be the problem?" Sandy told him angrily,

I'll miss my flight—it's my shoes and my UNDERWIRE, you morons!!!

Security called a police officer as Sandy continued to speak with hostility.

Sandy's communication style won her a complete search of her bags. The agent, who was very methodical and detailed in his search, seemed determined to find something incriminating in Sandy's bags. He was like a cat that had caught a mouse when he discovered a pair of tweezers. He said, "Ma'am, these are not authorized for carry-on. We will either need to confiscate these or you need to check your bag." Sandy's response was to say,

I have taken those tweezers through security in a hundred different airports. Will you tell me why they are suddenly a threat to our national security? I paid $20 for those tweezers, and surrendering them is not an option for me. I'll miss my flight. Just let me go!

Sandy ended up checking her bag and missing the earlier flight. She was in quite a mood when she called me. She wanted me to tell her, "I can't believe they treated you that way!" I wanted to say, "I can't believe you spoke to them that way!" She wanted me to tell her, "You should file a complaint!" I wanted to tell her, "I'm grateful they didn't put you in jail!"

Was Sandy justified to be angry? It's possible. It really doesn't matter if she was right or not. Her response only made the situation worse.

Remember: PowerPhrases get results. PowerPhrases are designed to work for you. Sandy spoke in a way that worked against her. Mark Twain has said, "Getting angry is easy. Anyone can do that. But getting angry in the right way in the right amount at the right time, now that's hard!"

Can you do that? Can you get angry at the right time, in the right way, and in the right amount? Polish off your Power-Phrases and you will! Be short, specific, targeted, and say what you mean and mean what you say, without being mean when you say it.

PowerPhrases to Express Anger Are Short

Passive people use too many words when they apologize for being upset in order to lighten their anger and soften the blow.

They express their anger in Respect-Robbing Poison Phrases. They'll say, "I'm sorry I'm angry," "I know you probably didn't mean it," "I might not be justified in saying this"—they will use qualifiers and disclaimers until no message is left.

Aggressive people use too many words because they want to drive the point in. They want to make sure the listener feels their anger.

Be sure all the relevant details are included, but don't go on and on. PowerPhrases are as long as they need to be and no longer.

PowerPhrases to Express Anger Are Specific

Get specific about the source of your anger and then get even more specific about the true nature of your anger. Avoid saying,

I'm angry because you don't listen.

when it's more specific to say,

I feel discounted because you ignored my warning.

Avoid saying,

I'm angry that I can't get through.

if it's more specific to say,

I'm frustrated because I have been on the phone for over forty minutes and shuffled from department to

department thirteen times and still don't have the person who can help me.

Avoid saying,

I'm mad that you're late.

when you mean,

I feel unvalued when you come twenty minutes late without calling.

Be specific about what they are doing that you want them to stop or what they are not doing that you want them to start. Be clear about what you think, feel, and want. They need to know how their behavior impacts you.

PowerPhrases to Express Anger Are Targeted

Like Sandy at the airport, you need to consider the consequences of your actions. Being justified isn't enough! Don't fight a battle you cannot win, and when the other person holds power, don't antagonize her. It's pretty simple. Ask yourself,

What result do I want and what words are likely to get that response?

Sandy wanted security to let her through and she wanted to catch her flight. Cursing was not the way to accomplish her goal, but that was the approach she chose. She had another goal—she also felt indignant about how they were searching her and she wanted them to stop. Had she understood the situation rationally, she would have weighed which goal mattered most and spoken accordingly. If the dominant goal was to catch her flight, saying nothing about her anger would probably have been the best approach. If she wanted to try to meet both goals, she might have done well to say,

I have underwire in my bra and that's what's setting the alarm off. I am embarrassed with the way you are touching me. Is there another way you can clear me that is less intrusive?

Would it have worked? I don't know. PowerPhrases don't always work, but they are always your best bet. I am certain that her chances for success would have been much greater than with the approach she took.

Express your anger, but don't sabotage your goals in the process. If telling them

I am furious about the oversight.

is likely to inspire them to be more attentive in the future, say it! If it is likely to create defensiveness, what is the point in expressing it?

No amount of indignity justifies speaking in a way that will backfire on you.

PowerPhrases to Express Anger Say What You Mean

Saying what you mean when you are angry can be tough, because when you are angry, you usually don't know what you think, feel, or want. You are in a fight-or-flight reaction. With all the blood rushing toward the major muscles, primed for action, there is very little blood left for thinking and problem-solving. Ask yourself,

What do I really mean? If I spoke without concern for how the other person heard it, what would I say?

That is your starting place. Go from there to balance what is in your heart and mind with what will get you what you want.
  Avoid saying,

That's okay, no problem.

when you mean

I am furious about this!

Avoid saying

It's a bit inconvenient when you fill the report out incorrectly.

when you mean

When the reports are filled in incorrectly it takes three hours out of my day to fix it, and I can't spare that time.

Avoid saying,

Is this absolutely necessary?

when you mean

I am embarrassed and feel violated.

The more closely your words match what's in your heart and the more authentic you are, the more powerful your words will be. Find what is in your heart and find a way to say just that—in words they can hear.

Be aware that anger is a secondary emotion. Often you think you are angry, but there are more vulnerable feelings underneath the emotion. I may be angry when my friend doesn't call, but what I really am feeling might be rejection. I might be angry when my sister doesn't appreciate the gift I gave her, but what I am really feeling might be guilt because I didn't take the time to pick out something special. Find your deepest meanings and decide which one will get you the best result.

PowerPhrases to Express Anger Mean What You Say

It is common to get angry when others don't respect what you say. Many parents say their kids don't cooperate until they hear their parents get angry and yell. There is an important unseen dynamic here. Do you ever say things you don't mean? For example, if you have kids, do you ever tell them to turn the television off and then ignore the fact that they haven't a half hour later? Then when you are finally serious about getting results, do you get angry? What happens when you do that is you teach people they don't have to pay attention to what you say until you get angry.

You can avoid getting angry altogether by meaning what you say before you get angry. You set yourself up to get angry if that is the only time you mean your words.

Avoid saying anything you have no intent to follow-up on. Ask yourself,

Do I really mean this? If I am tested, will I follow through?

Avoid saying,

I refuse to be searched like a common criminal.

if you don't have the power to refuse the search, and might have to submit.

Avoid saying,

If you show up late again, I'll leave.

if you don't plan to follow-through.

Avoid saying,

I'm going to report you.

if you have no idea how to do that and no intention to go to the trouble of finding out and taking action.

Meaning what you say when expressing anger is what makes your words work for you. Many people will shout empty threats at high volume, thinking they are speaking powerfully, while others have discovered quiet resolve to be much more effective. When you yell, you come across as being out of control. When you speak calmly, clearly, and mean every word you say, you sound in control.

When you need stronger PowerPhrases to communicate the

strength of your resolve, choose words to communicate consequences. Say,

If this doesn't change, I will . . .

I need as much specific information as you can give me, because I plan to discuss this with my attorney to see what my options are.

In order to be able to continue here I need . . .

The key ingredient is resolve. Your words are powerless if you do not mean what you say. Even if you do mean what you say, if you have a habit of saying things you don't mean, it is likely they won't believe you when you do.

PowerPhrases to Express Anger Are Not Mean When You Say Them

When people hurt, offend, or inconvenience you, it's natural to want to hurt, offend, or inconvenience them back. Tit for tat seems to be programmed into the human psyche. Tit for tat is also one of the stupidest things you can do.

It is possible to communicate anger without striking out in any way. It is also possible to communicate anger without judgment or blame. You do it by avoiding making the person you are angry at the target of your words. Instead of speaking about him, talk about his behavior or about how his behavior affects you.

Avoid saying,

You never tell me anything.

Say,

I am infuriated that I was not informed about the change in location.

Be aware: When you express yourself in PowerPhrases, it doesn't mean that no one will ever get hurt. Sometimes the honest and necessary expression of feelings can be hurtful, even when it is not expressed as an attack. You need to stand tall in the knowledge that you chose your words with respect, not venom.

The next time you become angry, power up, stand up, speak up, and SpeakStrong.

23

How to Disagree without Being Disagreeable

PowerPhrases to Handle Disagreements

When I teach seminars I rely on participation. If it was just me who talked, it would be a long day for us all.

I often pose questions to the group. Occasionally, the answers I get are not what I am looking for. Some answers are wrong. However, when someone answered a question, if I said,

That's wrong!

by the end of the day, I would have no participation. I don't want that to happen. I want to make it safe for members of my audience to offer their ideas. I make it safe to speak by finding what I can acknowledge in what people say.

I ask myself,

What about what they are saying could possibly be true?

Then I acknowledge whatever truth I find in their words before I make my point.

If someone in a seminar tells me,

If someone is rude or uses sarcasm with me, I just blow 'em away with my own sarcasm.

I won't argue even though I don't agree with that approach. Instead of saying,

That approach is moronic and Neanderthal.

I say,

I so understand the desire to do that. Let's talk about some of the risks.

Disagreeing without being disagreeable means finding the points you have in common and pointing them out before you express your own wisdom. PowerPhrases help. The way to disagree without being disagreeable is to acknowledge their position first.

PowerPhrases to Handle Disagreements Are Short

No one likes to be lectured. The more time you spend making your case, the more time they have to resist your case. There is a loss of face when you make your point in too many words. Instead of saying,

What you are suggesting couldn't possibly be true because of the following thirteen points in the policy and procedures manual. # 1 . . . , #2 . . . , etc. Janice knows you're wrong, because she said . . . and Frederick knows you're wrong because he said . . . and I talked to Joe, etc. . . . Then there is the news report that came out last Thursday that said . . .

use fewer words. Say,

You make some good points. Here are some guidelines in policy and procedures we'll want to consider.

A PowerPhrase is a long as it needs to be and no longer.

PowerPhrases to Handle Disagreements Are Specific

Say enough to make your point and stop. But be certain that the points you make are specific. Rather than saying,

Everyone knows that isn't true.

it is more specific to say,

I have information from Dr. Martin and Dr. Jones that we need to consider here.

Avoid saying,

We shouldn't use that vendor.

when you make your point better by saying,

> **That vendor isn't the best choice because they have a history of late shipments and charging for incidentals.**

Include all relevant details.

PowerPhrases to Handle Disagreements Are Targeted

Dr. Phil McGraw is famous for his phrase,

> **How's that working for you?**

He says people ramble on about how right they are in different situations and totally overlook the price of being right. If you disagree with someone, you need to do it in a way that will work for you. Ask yourself,

> **What outcome do I want from this conversation?**

> **What words are most likely to get me those results?**

Pick your battles. Ask yourself if the issue really matters. Does it really matter if they think there should be female announcers on the sidelines of football games or not? If it doesn't matter, let it go.

Once you decide it does matter, good conversation goals in disagreements are (1) gaining mutual understanding, (2) deciding on a perspective that you can both live with—either agreeing or "agreeing to disagree," (3) agreeing on a course of action.

Avoid being sidetracked into the mistaken goal of proving you are right and they are wrong. Don't allow your discussions to lose focus and become contests. When the discussion starts to feel like an argument, look for areas where the other person can be right. If you insist you are right, that makes her wrong. She immediately goes into proving how right she is.

First and foremost, avoid the Vicious Venom Poison Phrase,

You're wrong.

Even avoid,

I disagree.

They hear that the same as if you said they are wrong. Instead, say,

I see it differently.

That's one perspective. I have a different one.

You're right. My thoughts are . . .

That may be. What makes sense to me is . . .

You may be right. Let's look at the facts and see.

Help me to understand how you see it that way.

Can you clarify that?

That's an interesting perspective. What if . . .

Look for areas where you agree and confirm them. Say,

We are in agreement about a couple of things here . . .
(A) . . . and (B) . . . . Where we are still at odds is . . .

Helen was afraid she would be fired for losing an account. Before she brought up the subject of the account, she started with questions she knew her boss would answer "yes" to. She asked,

Is it true that I have been an asset to you for the majority of the five years I've been here?

Do you agree that my performance has improved within the last year?

I believe our relationship has been too valuable to end over a single incident that will never happen again. Do you agree?

Helen was delighted when she kept her job. Her comment was, "That works so much better than arguing."

Can you find things to agree with in a disagreement? You can if you try hard enough. It's worth it, because it works.

PowerPhrases to Handle Disagreements Say What You Mean

Leave out referring to universal principles when the real issue is subjective. For example, if someone's perfume is a problem for you, avoid saying,

People should consider others before they put on perfume.

say,

I'm sensitive to your perfume.

They can argue with the first statement; they can't argue with the second. They might not agree with your rule, but they can't argue with your preference.

If someone is gossiping don't say,

People shouldn't gossip.

say,

I'm uncomfortable talking about Judy when she's not here.

When you say what you really mean rather than reaching for rules, you avoid sounding self-righteous. That makes you more effective.

PowerPhrases to Handle Disagreements Mean What You Say

It's a PowerPhrase to say,

Let's find a way of looking at this that makes sense to both of us.

unless you mean

I'm going to say this to you, so you'll shut up and listen to my voice of superior reason.

It's a PowerPhrase to say,

That's an interesting perspective.

unless what you really mean is

That's ridiculous. Where did you get such a stupid idea?

It's a PowerPhrase to say

I want to hear your perspective on this.

—unless what you really mean is

Tell me what you think, so I can show you how ridiculous you are and how right I am.

Avoid implying that you are looking for consensus when you are really looking for ammunition. Your actions must back up your words or you will lose trust.

PowerPhrases to Handle Disagreements Are Not Mean When You Say Them

Ridicule people and watch them shut down. Honor their thoughts and watch them open up. When they open up to you, you can better understand their position. Understand their position, and you can integrate it with your own. There is power in being nice after all!

A wonderful formula for disagreeing is called the "feel-felt-found formula." You begin by acknowledging what they feel, explain that you or others have felt that way in the past, and explain what you have learned. For example, if someone doesn't want to use a credit card over the Internet, applying this formula you would say,

I understand how you feel. When I first used my credit card over the Internet, I felt nervous. When I found that it was actually safer than giving a credit card to a waiter, I felt better.

What a great way to disagree without being disagreeable!

Never, ever pass judgment on someone's idea when you want him to open up to your own. Do what works: Listen and speak in PowerPhrases.

24

Homicide Is Not an Option

Use PowerPhrases to Address Issues

Everyone has a nemesis. Everyone has one person who exists to make life miserable. Everyone has one person who knows every one of his buttons—and takes great delight in pressing them. Everyone has a person who makes it easier to understand the concept of homicide.

For Superman this person is Lex Luthor. For Laura Ingalls, it's Nellie Olsen. For Mindy, a sales manager, it was Brenda, her supervisor.

Brenda was a huge woman who had bright red hair and a personality to match. Some managers believe in management by objectives. Some managers believe in management by example. Brenda believed in management by intimidation. If you ever made a mistake, Brenda cut you down to size.

One day Mindy came back to the office and a woman

named Wendy was at her desk in tears. When Mindy asked what happened, Wendy responded, "What happened? I'll tell you what happened. Brenda is what happened. I came in $330 short of my goals and she told me in front of everyone at the sales meeting that I'm incompetent and should get a job sacking groceries. Mindy, I did my very best and I think I did a good job. I don't know how much longer I can work here."

That's when Mindy decided she needed to stand up for her office. Mindy decided to address her nemesis.

Mindy didn't just go barging into Brenda's office and have it out with her. Mindy did everything right. She went home and practiced what she was going to say. She stayed up until the small hours of the night, preparing her PowerPhrases.

When the morning came, Mindy thought she was prepared. Then she looked down and saw that her socks didn't match and her top was not only on inside-out but backwards as well. There was no time to fix anything—Brenda walked in. Mindy stood a bit taller than usual to compensate for her fear and said,

Brenda, I need five minutes of your time to discuss an issue. Is now a good time?

Brenda's eyebrows lifted and she said, "Yeah!"

When they got into the conference room, Brenda closed the door behind her. Her eyes narrowed as she asked,

What's up?

Mindy responded,

Brenda, the monthly sales meetings are creating problems. People are afraid of you when you reprimand

them. I know when you chastise them at your sales meetings for falling short of their goals your purpose is to get them to try harder. It has the opposite effect. It makes them want to quit. Several times people have broken down in tears. I believe if they had encouragement and guidance from you they would not only be motivated to do better. They would know what to do.

Brenda's voice rose as she said,

So Mindy, you are telling me that I don't know what I am doing? And, Mindy, you are saying that you do? Mindy, you are not the supervisor here. I am. You stick to your job and I'll stick to mine.

Mindy responded,

I understand why it might sound like I am telling you how to do your job. It's not my intention to do that. I want to keep the good people we have here. I believe encouragement and support from you would make the difference.

Then Mindy turned and walked out.

There was nothing in Mindy's conversation with Brenda to indicate how successful her conversation was. Time told that story.

One month later, a woman named Karen fell $425 short of her goals. She and her coworkers were astonished at the sales meeting when Brenda said,

We had a good month. Karen, you were a bit short, but pretty close. I have some ideas that might help you meet

your goals next month, because I want to see you be successful.

How about you? Who is your nemesis? Who is the one person who knows every one of your buttons—and takes great delight in pressing them? Who is the one person who makes it easier to understand the concept of homicide?

For Mindy it was Brenda. Mindy found a way to be completely clear while still being respectful of Brenda. You can be clear and respectful at the same time. Take inspiration from Mindy. Take yourself off mute and address your nemesis with PowerPhrases. Be short, specific, targeted, say what you mean, mean what you say, and don't be mean when you say it.

PowerPhrases to Address Issues Are Short

Mindy used enough words to be clear, but eliminated excess words. She resisted the temptation to "get it over with quickly," but she also resisted the temptation to over-explain. Every word she used worked toward her goal in speaking.

PowerPhrases to Address Issues Are Specific

Mindy's message was specific enough for Brenda to know exactly what behavior caused problems. She was specific about four areas:

1. She told Brenda exactly what behavior she wanted changed. She didn't say,

Be a nicer manager.

She wasn't trying to turn Brenda into an ideal manager. She took a specific approach to addressing issues. She wanted to get Brenda to replace her criticisms at the monthly meetings with praise and guidance. Mindy said,

> **Brenda, the monthly sales meetings are creating problems. People are afraid of you when you chastise them.**

2. Mindy made the impact of Brenda's words clear. She didn't say,

> *It doesn't feel good.*

She said,

> **It makes them want to quit. Several times people have broken down in tears.**

3. Mindy acknowledged Brenda.

> **I know your purpose is to get them to try harder.**

4. Mindy made it clear what she wanted Brenda to do instead.

> **I believe if they had encouragement and guidance from you they would not only be motivated to do better. They would know what to do.**

When you address your nemesis and tackle issues that you have been avoiding, be specific about the behavior you want to see changed, how the behavior is affecting you or the company, what you appreciate about her or her perspective, and what behavior you want her to embrace.

PowerPhrases to Address Issues Are Targeted

Mindy had two goals in this conversation. Her primary goal was to get Brenda to stop being so harsh in meetings. Her second goal was to keep her job. She succeeded in both.

Mindy may have been tempted to argue when Brenda accused Mindy of telling her how to do her job. She didn't. Instead she said,

> **I understand why it might sound like I am telling you how to do your job. It's not my intention to do that.**

Had she argued with Brenda's accusations, she would have started an argument that she couldn't win. She would have gotten off track from the results she wanted.

Remember to ask yourself,

> **What specific outcome do I want to achieve?**

> **What words are most likely to get me there?**

Make certain that your suggestions consider the other person's needs and goals as well as your own. Stay focused on your desired result and the words that will get you there.

PowerPhrases to Address Issues Say What You Mean

What would you say if you did not edit yourself? What do you really mean? What do you think? What do you feel? What do you want? Why is their behavior a problem? That is where you start finding the words. Then balance those words with what is likely to get results.

Many times people will write me or come to me with specific questions about what to say when they address an issue. I usually find the perfect words in their own words. Listen to what you are telling others. You will find the words to communicate with your nemesis in those words.

PowerPhrases to Address Issues Mean What You Say

Only say things you intend to follow through with. Mindy might have chosen to say,

If this continues, I will speak to the supervisor about it.

That would be a PowerPhrase if she believed she needed that strong of communication and if she meant it. Only say it if you mean it.

PowerPhrases to Address Issues Are Not Mean When You Say Them

As out-of-line as Brenda may have seemed, Mindy did not utter one word of attack or say one thing that challenged Brenda's dignity. It does not matter how me-against-you she tries to make it. When you see the situation as the two of you against a problem—when you refuse to view her as your adversary—when you preserve her dignity no matter how vehemently she attacks yours—you preserve your own dignity as well and you get RESULTS.

Because a PowerPhrase is as strong as it needs to be and no stronger, you will want to start gently and if that isn't getting results, use stronger words.

I prefer.

is not as strong as

I want.

I want is not as strong as

I need.

When you need to speak more strongly yet, add consequences. Say,

I will.

Who is your nemesis? Everyone has one! Polish off your Power-Phrases and address the issue.

25

What He Says Is Not What She Hears and What She Says Is Not What He Hears

PowerPhrases between the Genders

This information was circulating through the Internet:

> A man turned to his wife and said, "Honey, it says that the average man speaks 15,000 words a day and the average woman speaks 30,000 words a day!"
>
> His wife replied, "That's because we have to repeat everything."
>
> The man said, "What?"

If it is true that men aren't hearing women, it might not be entirely their fault. It might be that women are speaking a different language. If women use twice as many words as men do, perhaps men lose the message buried in too many words.

According to gender communication expert Deborah Tannen, research shows that men speak more than women in professional settings, such as meetings and presentations. This is partially because women wait to be "given the floor" and men do not. Women speak more in personal settings, such as at dinner and at home.

Another gender difference is that men speak impersonally, while women speak personally. A man is likely to be more interested in an article in the *New York Times* about how college kids behave, while a woman would relate more to a discussion of her niece's and nephew's behavior.

Another difference in communication between the genders is that men tend to be more literal. Women hint more. If someone says, "I hope I have enough help at the conference," a woman might interpret the remark as a request for help. A man is less likely to hear a request that was not deliberately stated.

Men build bonds by testing and challenging each other. Women build bonds by finding areas of similarity. When I tell men that I am an expert on PowerPhrases, they are likely to challenge what I know and tell me what they know about communication. Their approach is not intended to be disrespectful in any way; in fact, it is a sign of respect. Women are more likely to inquire into what I know.

So how do we talk to each other? In PowerPhrases, of course!

PowerPhrases between the Genders Are Short

Be brief in speaking with men and women—but a bit briefer with the men than with the women. Men are used to very quick conversations, such as,

Lunch?

Yeah.

12:30 P.M.—Joe's Diner.

For women this may sound too abrupt as they are more inclined to say,

It's been a long time since we had lunch together. Would today work for you?

Sure! I was going to have lunch with Mary, but she cancelled.

Really. Why did she cancel? (etc.)

Many men communicate on a need-to-know basis. If they don't think you need to know something, they'll see no reason to communicate. As a woman, I was amazed that when one of my son's friends was fired from his job, none of his male coworkers found out why. The subject never came up. They saw no need to know. Women would be far more likely to want to discuss all aspects of the situation. Don't personalize those differences. It isn't personal!

A male coworker used to be silent when I spoke. I thought he hadn't heard me, so I would repeat myself. He heard me— he didn't have anything to say. He learned to say something like

That's right.

Interesting.

just so I knew he had heard me. Men are more inclined to understand a silent response than women are. Add a few more words for communicating with women, and don't personalize the brevity of men. In all situations, a PowerPhrase is as long as it needs to be and no longer.

PowerPhrases between the Genders Are Specific

This PowerPhrases Principle is particularly important to women communicating with men, since men tend to be more literal.

Women: It is important for women to be specific about the reason for a conversation with men. If a woman wants a man to listen and not try to fix a problem, she needs to tell him so. Say,

I'm upset about something and want to talk. All I need from you is your ear.

If a woman wants help solving a problem, she needs to say,

I need your help to solve a problem.

Don't expect men to guess what you want. Tell them specifically. For example, I once sent a copy of a book I published to a male colleague. I told him,

When you get your copy of the book, I want you to tell me the cover is beautiful.

He replied,

Thanks for telling me exactly what you want from me.

To be specific avoid saying,

We never go anywhere.

when you mean,

Please take me to Alexander's Restaurant tonight.

Men, if you ever wonder what a woman wants from you, ask! Say,

How can I best support you? Do you want me to just listen, or help you solve this?

If a woman is generalizing, avoid picking at the literal meaning of what she is saying. If she says, "We never go out," do not respond by saying,

That's not true! We went out last week.

Ask yourself what the specific need is behind the remark and speak to that. Say,

Do you want to go out tonight?

If she says, "I do all the work around here," do not respond to her literal words by saying,

You're wrong. Why just yesterday I sent a fax for you.

Again, ask yourself what she specifically means and speak to that.

Do you need some help right now?

Rather than respond to the literal meaning of her words, ask yourself how you can get to the specific nature of the issue. PowerPhrases are specific.

PowerPhrases between the Genders Are Targeted

To get results, speak more impersonally with men and more personally with women. Want to persuade a man to see a movie you want to see? Tell him,

The reviews were unanimously positive. It received four Academy Award nominations.

Want to get a woman to see a movie you want to see? Say,

I heard that Barbara and Susan saw it and loved it.

Do you want to be taken seriously? If you are speaking to a group with men in it, be sure to include factual data.

A recent survey shows that 25 percent of our children are being raised by a single parent.

If you are speaking to a group with women in it, be certain to add the human touch.

When the judge asked Sean which parent he wanted to live with, he said, "I just want everything to go back to being the way it was."

If your goal in a communication is to be respected, avoid dwelling on your problems in speaking with men. Women see this as a bonding signal, but men see it as a sign of weakness.

Be aware that men primarily speak to relay information, while women also speak to build rapport and sort out their thoughts. Know what kind of results you are looking for, understand the purpose of speaking, and communicate that purpose to your listener so they know how to listen and you get the results you want.

PowerPhrases between the Genders Say What You Mean

Often women will disguise opinions as questions. For example, a woman who believes a bid is too high might say,

Do you think we can do better?

She needs to say what she means. She needs to say,

This bid is too high. We can do better.

Men are more literal and less likely to take hints than women. Author Mimi Donaldson says that if a woman comments,

I love flowers.

the man does not assume she is suggesting he get her some. Mimi suggests women do better to ask directly,

Please get me 13 yellow roses for my birthday. Here's the store I want you to get them from.

When I share this example in mixed groups, the women moan and the men love it! "Say what you mean!" they exclaim.

With men, be sure that you say what you mean by stressing the objective sides of your points. Say,

The restructuring will impact us in the following three ways.

With women, when you say what you mean, include some personal information.

When I first heard about the restructuring, I wondered how it would affect the security of my coworkers' positions.

There are many ways to say what you mean, so pick the meaning that will get better results.

PowerPhrases between the Genders Mean What You Say

Women tend to exaggerate more than men do. A woman might say, "That's a blouse to die for!" But a man is unlikely to say, "That's a tie to die for!" A woman might say, "It cost a fortune," whereas a man is more likely to say, "It cost $332, which was about $80 more than I expected."

This difference in communication can create false expectations. For example, a woman might say, "I'll make sure everyone is at the meeting," meaning she'll get as many people as she can, and a man is likely to be surprised if one or two people aren't there.

Be sure you mean what you say. Women, ask yourself if you literally mean what you are saying. If you are communicating with a man, express yourself in more concrete terms.

Women also tend to share passing thoughts while men are more likely to say things they've thought about for a while. A woman might share a passing thought and be surprised when a man thought she meant it. If a woman says, "My job is doing me in," a man is likely to assume she means it and suggest other jobs. Women, again, ask yourself if you really mean what you are saying.

PowerPhrases between the Genders Are Not Mean When You Say Them

For too long, women have been criticized for their sensitivity and men have been criticized for their lack of it. There is a Tim Allen comedy routine about his wife's car running out of oil. He asks, "Didn't the oil light go on?" She replies, "Why yes, it did!" He responds,

Tell me, how did you FEEL about that?

While this kind of sarcastic ridicule is funny in the abstract, it can be very painful in life.

Men, if someone is emoting and you need to get them to focus on the facts, do so without being critical in any way. Avoid saying,

Don't give me any of that emotional garbage. Just tell me you'll be on time.

say,

I understand that you are facing personal challenges and, of course, that will affect your work. I am faced with the problem that I need someone at your station on time. How can we make that happen?

Women, be aware that men use sports, military, and sexual jargon in their conversations more than women. It is very helpful for women to learn the language and use it, with the exclusion of sexual jargon.

Women, if a man makes a joke that you find offensive, object without passing judgment. Instead of saying,

I am shocked that you would find that funny. What, were you raised in a bar?

say,

That kind of humor offends me.

Draw boundaries when something offends you. But it is also important not to be judgmental about a style of conversation that is considered acceptable among the other gender.

Do men and women speak different languages? I say it's more like different dialects. Learn the dialect of your counterpart, and enjoy the communication that results.

Part 4

Put Your Best Self Forward with PowerPhrases

26

Tips for Using PowerPhrases

Now that you have a deeper understanding of PowerPhrases, let's look at some tips that will help you use your PowerPhrases more effectively.

Tip #1: It's Not What You Say—It's How You Say It

You've heard it said before. It's true. If you say,

I need this by 3:00 P.M.

—in a passive tone of voice, it becomes a Respect-Robbing Poison Phrase that weakens. If you say the same thing in an aggressive tone of voice, it becomes a Vicious Venom Poison Phrase that hurts. If you say,

I'm sure glad you're here.

in a sarcastic tone, that perfectly positive statement becomes poison!

When you use your PowerPhrases, imagine you are asking someone to pass the butter. When you ask someone to pass the butter, it's no big deal unless you live in a very strange house. Keep your voice as calm as when you ask for butter. If you choose to add intensity, do it in a way so you still come across as being calm.

I had someone get upset with me who was telling me in great detail what I had done that bothered her. It was several minutes into the conversation before I realized that she was angry, and I was not feeling a need to defend myself. I wasn't feeling defensive because she used a calm, non-threatening tone of voice. As a result, I was able to listen to the specifics of her upset rather than reacting to the emotion of her expression.

Tip #2: Sometimes Silence Is Golden

Pick your battles and decide when to and when not to speak. Just because you have PowerPhrases doesn't mean you need to address every issue. When I ask couples who have been together for a long time to explain their secret, they often tell me that they overlook a lot. If you are truly bothered by something, it is important for you to speak up, but you don't need to speak up about everything that is not to your individual liking.

Silence is golden when,

1. It doesn't matter that much.

2. You are too triggered to speak rationally.

3. Your words are unlikely to bring a good result.

My friend and client Bill had a golden silence. He was recently sitting next to his mother at his son's wedding. Bill commented on how hot the room was. His mother argued, "Hot? It's cold." Bill replied, "I guess that's because you're just wearing a dress and I'm wearing a jacket, vest, shirt, and undershirt." Bill's mother countered with "You're wearing a jacket, vest, shirt, undershirt, and a layer of fat." Bill silently got up and went to another part of the church.

Bill was wise to not just ignore the nastiness of the comment at the moment. Bill also was wise to avoid arguing with his mother at the church. His silence spoke volumes. He does have an ongoing issue with his mother that needs to be addressed, but the wedding was neither the time nor the place. His mother got his silent message and later apologized.

Tip #3: Don't Expect the World to Communicate in PowerPhrases

Most people do not have good communication skills. If someone says something to you that triggers you, ask yourself how he might have said it more effectively. In your mind, translate his words into PowerPhrases and respond to the real issue rather than the issue of how he said it.

When a video editor told me

I hate your script.

I translated his remark into

I have some recommendations for your script.

and we proceeded amicably.

Tip #4: In Some Situations No PowerPhrase Will Help

Someone said to me, "PowerPhrases sound great in an ideal world, but in the real world it doesn't work like that." My experience shows me that PowerPhrases do work in the real world— most of the time, at least. PowerPhrases are designed for the imperfect world of imperfect people we live in and live with.

Of course, there are situations beyond reason. Occasionally, people will come to me with questions that sound as if they are asking me how to turn a sociopath into a normal person. I do not have tools to do that.

You will sometimes encounter situations in which no matter how well-worded your PowerPhrases are, the cards are stacked against you. Your best option is damage control by removing yourself from these unhealthy situations.

There will always be people who continue to drink alcohol long after their seizures cause them to lose their jobs, no matter what you tell them. There will always be people who try the next get-rich-quick scheme after losing their inheritance in the last one, no matter how well-worded your warnings are. You will always have those friends who date Ms. or Mr. Wrong, no matter whom you try to set them up with. People need to learn their own lessons.

PowerPhrases can't change other people. PowerPhrases can influence other people, however—and PowerPhrases can totally transform you. I do not recommend giving up on a situation until you have used PowerPhrases to your best ability. I do recommend retreating from a war you can never win.

Tip #5: Learn and Practice the Runion Rules for Communication

I have eight guidelines that I call the Runion Rules, because the word "rules" sounds so nice with my last name! I commit to these and recommend you do as well.

1. Pass Up Points at a Price

Never score points at someone else's expense. It will come back to get you.

2. Swear Off Sarcasm

Eliminate sarcasm except when there is a high degree of trust and you are certain that no one will be offended.

3. Banish the Beam in Your Own Eye First

When you do not like how someone is communicating with you, before you speak ask yourself how the way you are communicating might be contributing to the way she speaks.

4. Judge Ye Not

Eliminate judgment from your words. Know the difference between discernment and judgment.

5. Know Their Needs

When someone else needs to talk, it's your turn to listen—even if it's not REALLY your turn to listen. (There are occasional exceptions to this rule.)

6. Balance Your Power

Speak as strongly as you need to and no stronger.

7. Remember 24-Hour Power

Remember the 24-hour rule. If you feel compelled to say something that carries a risk, wait 24 hours before you open your mouth.

8. Use Your Verbal Litmus Test

Evaluate your words by the six PowerPhrase Principles before you speak. If your words don't fit all six, rework them. These principles are: (1) Short, (2) Specific, (3) Targeted, (4) Say what you mean, (5) Mean what you say, (6) Don't be mean when you say it.

Tip #6: "A PowerPhrase a Week" Newsletter Is Your Secret Weapon

You develop new skills through repetition. "A PowerPhrase a Week" is a free weekly e-mail newsletter that enables you to review the PowerPhrase Principles one week at a time, to hear how others are using the principles, and to get your particular questions answered. Send an e-mail to Subscribe@SpeakStrong. com. You will see a sample copy at the back of this book.

These tips add muscle to your PowerPhrases. Keep them firmly in mind.

27

Answers to Readers' Most Pressing, Vexing, and Perplexing Communication Questions

My readers enjoy the question/answer column in my weekly e-mail newsletters. Here are some of the most pressing, vexing, and perplexing problems readers bring to me—and my responses.

Question #1: How to Be a New Manager without Being Considered an "Occupying Power"

Dear Meryl: I am writing to ask for some ideas on how to deal with being an employee in a new job situation. I was just hired as a dietary manager for a small-town nursing home. Most of the staff has been working there since the dawn of time. I will have about ten folks to supervise. I don't want them to think I am going to change the world, but I do want them to know that I am going to listen to what they have to say about how things have been run in their kitchen. Apparently, there are some issues regarding overtime hours and the budget for them. I would like to have a staff meeting soon to introduce my position and to find out about theirs. Any suggestions would be greatly appreciated.

Meryl Responds: It is always difficult to take over as a supervisor. Tell them what you are telling me:

> I am aware many of you have been here for a long time. I want to be certain to draw on your expertise. I want to be certain I understand what is and isn't working before we look for new ways of doing anything.

Then learn about them. Ask,

Are there obstacles you see that make it challenging to do your job?

What can I do to make your job easier?

What motivates you?

What do you like about this job?

What do you not like about this job?

Next, tell them a bit about you and your vision. You are wise to realize it's important to fully understand how things work and win trust before you make too many changes. These phrases will help.

Question #2: Keep It Down to a Dull Roar

Dear Meryl: I have a friend at work who needs to communicate a problem with one of our coworkers. This coworker can be very unapproachable, as she is a VERY negative person. The problem is that she has been receiving personal phone calls from a bill collector here at work. (The ironic thing is that we work in an accounts receivable department. Funny, huh?) Whenever she receives one of these calls, she gradually starts getting louder and louder. When this happens, my friend cannot hear whom she is talking to on the phone. Not to mention, after [the coworker] hangs up she rants and raves about the conversation. We are in dire need of a PowerPhrase!!! Can you help?

Meryl Responds: You and your friend need to be a united force when expressing your concerns to this coworker. The words you choose must be straightforward. Say,

> I wonder if you are aware how loud your voice gets. It actually interferes with my ability to hear my own conversation and I'm concerned that the other party hears you as well. I am aware that the situation is upsetting to you; however, we need you to keep your voice low.

When she resists, don't argue or try to convince her. Simply say,

I understand this is upsetting to you. Your volume affects our ability to do our job.

If she is as negative as you say, she will probably take a potshot at you. Let her. Your goal is to get her to stop speaking so loud, so let her have her reaction as you take consistent action towards your goal. Stay calm in vocal tone, firm in resolve, and speak up after every incident. Say what you mean and mean what you say.

Question #3: Her Right to Smell Good vs. My Right to Breathe

Dear Meryl: I appreciate your PowerPhrase e-mails. They help me so much! I'm hoping you can help with a problem I have. One particular female coworker (who sits real close to my desk) likes to load up with perfume. It is very strong, and sometimes I have a hard time breathing when it drifts to my desk. She has an office with a door, and I do not, so sometimes I turn my desk fan away from me so that I don't have to inhale the strong perfume. I really like her and do not wish to offend her. Can you help me?

Meryl Responds: I bet this woman has no idea that her perfume is a problem and she won't know unless you tell her. I would simply say,

I'm sensitive to perfume and it affects my breathing. Would you mind using a little less?

Keep it short, simple, and unapologetic. You have every right to let her know that her perfume is a problem. If she chooses to take offense, it is her choice.

You can have your PowerPhrases questions answered by e-mailing Questions@SpeakStrong.com.

28

Oh, My Gosh! PowerPhrases Really Work!

Success Stories from the Field

PowerPhrases are real and they are for the real world. I receive e-mails daily about successes people have had when they take themselves off of mute and SpeakStrong. I am sharing a few with you so you will know that PowerPhrases are no abstraction. They are real.

PowerPhrases to Get the Boss to See the Good

Dear Meryl: About a month ago I went through a review process with my employer. The objectives were to discuss my past year and to explain what my goals were for the next year. During that process, my employer made it quite clear that he wanted me to take more of a "leadership" role and help lead the company in the areas of my expertise.

A portion of my job is financial and a week before my review I had completed a four-month process of redeveloping our financial model and constructing our budget for 2003. When I presented him the completed budget, I expected him to be pleased that I resolved the discrepancies and completed it on time. He quickly noted some small items that I hadn't modified for the forthcoming year and began to pick apart my report, explaining to me that leadership meant presenting to him an "error free" report.

I explained during my review that I realized I had made mistakes and took responsibility for them. I assured him that I wouldn't make those mistakes again. I also mentioned that he knew that I had worked very hard on the project, and that I was expecting him to to be pleased because it was complete. I said that I was taken aback by his remarks on my errors.

He said (very sincerely), "Y'know, you're absolutely right. I am sorry. You did work long and hard on that project and did complete it on time. Thank you."

I sat there graciously receiving his compliment, but inside I was stunned that what I said had the impact it did.

PowerPhrases to Gain Respect

Dear Meryl: When I first started with my company, I was working on recruitment. I was extremely sick and took a lot of time off during the first six months. Many administrative assistants didn't respect the fact that I needed to take so much time off from work and had a real attitude toward me.

After ten months with the company, I was promoted to a support manager role within my team. Knowing this would cause some tension, I took each of my team members aside and spoke to them about the varying reasons for conflict. I told one team member, Dana, in particular:

I understand that in the past we have had our difference of opinions. Due to my promotion we will be working closer together. We don't have to be friends outside of work, but if we can work together in a harmonious and supportive environment, that would be good not only for me, but for the entire team.

Dana spoke to me the following morning and said that for the first time since I'd started, she respected me. She stayed with the company another six months and then left to travel overseas. In her final months with the company, Dana had created a pleasant work environment within the company. As a result, everyone on our team saw that it was possible for us to all get along.

A PowerPhrase to Balance the Workload

Dear Meryl: With the economic crunch, my duties have been continually increased. Recently, my supervisor volunteered us for another time-consuming duty. When he came to my office to tell me I would have to tackle this new task and said, "You will make this work easily and efficiently as you have with your other duties . . . ," I let him ramble on about how he would like to see procedures and policies to enhance our task. When he was finished and asked me for my input, I found he had opened a door for me.

I asked,

What duties do you see as having priority over these I currently have?

I let him list off the tasks he knew were the most important. When he completed his list, I asked,

Which duty could I delegate to have the appropriate time to make this new project successful?

He stared at me dumbfounded for almost an entire minute (47 seconds as I watched the clock above his head) before he answered "None."

I then told him that in light of making this project have a smooth conversion to our area I did not feel I could give it the time and attention with my current duties. I asked how we might be able to split the duties between some of our personnel who are always asking for projects to do to pass the time better. We talked for another 15 minutes before we had a plan written out on what needed to be done, when the tasks needed to happen, and who could do the tasks. We have made the conversion and things are running fairly smooth.

My supervisor mentioned the other day that he now sees why I resisted to take on this task because he spends a minimum of 10 hours a week with his portion of the tasks and sees that I could not have done this without giving up 2 to 3 tasks I currently have.

I am quite proud that I was able to tell him NO without

using the N word, as I feel this is a negative word when not used properly.

What success stories do you have? Send your success stories to Success@SpeakStrong.com. In return, we will send you a free "Pippi SpeakStrong" giraffe!

29

Your PowerPhrases
Final Exam

We've come a long way together. It's time to find out what you have learned. Your PowerPhrases Final Exam follows. Once you reach the end, check your answers against mine.

1. Under what three circumstances is silence not golden?

2. How many times more likely are you to tell a provider you don't like a service than that you do?

3. What is the main reason managers dread performance reviews—and how can PowerPhrases help?

4. What is the definition of "power"?

5. What is the definition of a PowerPhrase?

6. What is a Vicious Venom Poison Phrase?

7. What is a Respect-Robbing Poison Phrase?

8. List three filler Respect-Robbing Poison Phrases.

9. List three qualifier Respect-Robbing Poison Phrases.

10. List three indecisive Respect-Robbing Poison Phrases.

11. List three vague, hinting Respect-Robbing Poison Phrases.

12. List three negative, weakening Respect-Robbing Poison Phrases.

13. List three labeling Vicious Venom Poison Phrases.

14. List three absolute Vicious Venom Poison Phrases.

15. List three negative Vicious Venom Poison Phrases that maim.

16. What are three more types of Vicious Venom Poison Phrases that can overpower and maim?

17. How many words are contained in the Gettysburg Address?

18. Fill in the blank. If your conscious mind does not choose a goal for a conversation, your _____ will.

19. What are four valuable goals to strive for in using Power-Phrases?

20. If you don't mean it don't _____ it.

21. Give two reasons why small talk is important.

22. To get a conversation going, give your listener a little extra _____.

23. What is the main key to small talk?

24. Always be certain to express _____ as thoughts and _____ as feelings.

25. Is this a legitimate feeling: I feel you should have called?

26. List three key PowerPhrases for making powerful requests.

27. What are the three parts of PowerPhrases for saying "no"?

28. List three key PowerPhrases for listening.

29. What three things should you disclose to apologize successfully?

30. What are five types of PowerPhrase questions?

31. What is the definition of "manipulation"?

32. List three examples of improper uses of questions.

33. What are the three reasons people use sarcasm or mixed messages?

34. Defusing anger is as much about what you _____ do as what you do.

35. What distinction do you need to make in determining what makes you angry?

36. Get specific about the _____ of your anger and the _____ of your anger.

37. What two questions must you ask yourself when using PowerPhrases to handle disagreements?

38. List three key PowerPhrases to handle disagreements.

39. List three key PowerPhrases to handle conflict.

40. Name three differences in the way men and women communicate.

41. What do you pretend you are asking for in order to sound calm when speaking in PowerPhrases?

42. In what kinds of situations is silence golden?

43. What is the e-mail address to send your PowerPhrase questions and PowerPhrase success stories?

Answers to Exam

Your PowerPhrases Final Exam follows with the answers. Let's see how you did.

1. Under what three circumstances is silence not golden?

   1. When you have information they need, even if they don't want to hear it.

   2. When they need to know you care.

   3. When they need to be kept in the loop.

2. How many times more likely are you to tell a provider you don't like a service than that you do?

   Ten times.

3. What is the main reason managers dread performance reviews—and how can PowerPhrases help?

   They don't realize they can use them (1) as an opportunity to point out what went well in the preceding period, and (2) as a time to set goals.

4. What is the definition of "power"?

   The ability to get results.

5. What is the definition of a PowerPhrase?

A short, specific, targeted expression that says what you mean and means what you say without being mean when you say it.

6. What is a Vicious Venom Poison Phrase?

   Vicious Venom Poison Phrases are destructive and harmful phrases.

7. What is a Respect-Robbing Poison Phrase?

   Respect-Robbing Poison Phrases are phrases that weaken your message.

8. List three filler Respect-Robbing Poison Phrases.

   Here are four: *Well, um, you know, like.*

9. List three qualifier Respect-Robbing Poison Phrases.

   Here are several: *I sort of, I just, I'm wondering if, it kind of, it seems like, I could be wrong but, this is just a thought I'm having, sorry to bother you, I have one little question, maybe we could.*

10. List three indecisive Respect-Robbing Poison Phrases.

    Did you have any of these? *I should, I'll try, I might be able to, maybe we could, you might want to consider, one possibility might be, perhaps.*

11. List three vague, hinting Respect-Robbing Poison Phrases.

I wish someone would, I could use some help around here, I might want your help with . . .

12. List three negative, weakening Respect-Robbing Poison Phrases.

    Here are some examples: *I'll have to, I can't, it doesn't, I'm not good at, if only, but.*

13. List three labeling Vicious Venom Poison Phrases.

    Here are five: *You're an idiot, you're a bully, you're selfish, you're a bad listener, you're cheap.*

14. List three absolute Vicious Venom Poison Phrases.

    Here are four: *Always, never, every time, everything.*

15. List three negative Vicious Venom Poison Phrases that maim.

    Don't, no, you can't.

16. What are three more types of Vicious Venom Poison Phrases that can overpower and maim?

    The "shoulds," veiled assumptions, and assumed intentions.

17. How many words are contained in the Gettysburg Address?

18. Fill in the blank. If your conscious mind does not choose a goal for a conversation, your _____ will.

Unconscious.

19. What are four valuable goals to strive for in using Power-Phrases?

    1. To understand the other person,

    2. to express yourself so he understands you,

    3. to problem-solve, and

    4. to relay needed information.

20. If you don't mean it, don't _____ it.

Say.

21. Give two reasons why small talk is important.

    1. Big things begin with small talk,

    2. It's not what you know, but who you know.

22. To get a conversation going, give your listener a little extra _____.

Information about yourself.

23. What is the main key to small talk?

Without getting too personal, ignore the artificial barriers between you and the other person and speak as if you already know him.

24. Always be certain to express _____ as thoughts and _____ as feelings.

Thoughts; feelings.

25. Is this a legitimate feeling: I feel that you should have called?

No—it's a thought.

26. List three key PowerPhrases for making powerful requests.

Here are a few examples:

I need your help.

Can you do that for me?

How can we make that happen?

What would it take for you to be able to _____ for me?

Will you . . . ?

27. What are the three parts of PowerPhrases for saying "no"?

1. Acknowledgment of their request,

2. a brief explanation of why you can't or won't, and

3. a tag to affirm the relationship or an alternative recommendation.

28. List three key PowerPhrases for listening.

    Did you list any of these?

    I want to hear what you have to say.

    I didn't know you felt that way.

    I see why that would be an issue for you.

    I can imagine how that might have felt.

    Tell me more.

    What else can you tell me about that?

    That's an interesting point.

    What did you like about that?

    Help me to understand.

    I'm a bit confused about . . .

    What were you referring to when you said . . . ?

    I didn't catch something you said a minute ago.

    **Let me make sure I understand what you are saying.
    I believe you are saying . . .**

    So when _____ happened you felt _____ ?

    What you need from me is. . . . Am I right?

    I appreciate you being so open with me.

    You can talk to me.

    I want to hear what you have to say.

29. What three things should you disclose to apologize successfully?

1. The words "I'm sorry,"

2. acknowledgment of how you harmed the other person, and

3. a direct request that he or she pardon or excuse you.

30. What are five types of PowerPhrase questions?

Here are six!

1. To get the listener involved. Most of my questions in this book are to get you thinking and involved.

2. To find out what they know.

3. To see if they mean what they are saying.

4. To make sure you were clear with them.

5. To gather information.

6. To regain the balance of control in a conversation.

31. What is the definition of "manipulation"?

To play upon or control by artful, unfair, or insidious means.

32. List three examples of improper uses of questions.

Here are four possible answers:

1. Questions that set them up.

2. Questions to control a conversation.

3. Leading questions that manipulate them into saying what you want them to say.

4. Questions that seem like interrogations.

33. What are the three reasons people use sarcasm or mixed messages?

    1. They are just plain mean and they have been getting away with it,

    2. they have a real concern and don't know how to address the issue directly, and

    3. it is a habit they are unaware of.

Whatever reason, the cure is the same: PowerPhrases!

34. Defusing anger is as much about what you _____ do as what you do.

    Don't.

35. What distinction do you need to make in determining what makes you angry?

    What is a short-term reaction and what are the deeper feelings underneath that reaction.

36. Get specific about the _____ of your anger and the _____ of your anger.

Source; true nature.

37. What two questions must you ask yourself when using PowerPhrases to handle disagreements?

   1. What outcome do I want from this conversation?

   2. What wors are most likely to get me those results?

38. List three key PowerPhrases to handle disagreements.

   Here are several:

   You're right, and I have a different opinion.

   I see it differently.

   That's one perspective. I have a different one.

   You're right. My thoughts are . . .

   That may be. What makes sense to me is . . .

   You may be right. Let's look at the facts and see.

   Help me to understand how you see it that way.

   Can you clarify that?

   That's an interesting perspective. What if. . . ?

   It looks like we are in agreement about a couple of things here . . . A) . . . and B) . . . . Where we are still at odds is . . . .

39. List three key PowerPhrases to handle conflict.

Did you have any of these?

There is an issue I'd like to discuss. Can we meet?

_____ is creating problems.

The effect is . . .

I/we feel . . .

What happens is . . .

I understand . . .

I appreciate . . .

I want . . .

I need . . .

I prefer . . .

That may be.

I see this is a big issue for you.

I didn't realize that was an issue for you.

How can we make this work for both of us?

What can I do to make you want to give me what I want here?

Let's see if we can find a solution that works for both of us.

Let's implement what we've decided and review how well it's working.

40. Name three differences in the way men and women communicate.

Here are four:

1. Men speak more in public settings while women speak more in social settings.

2. Men are more literal while women use more generalizations.

3. Men speak on a more factual and objective level while women speak on a more personal and subjective level.

4. Men build bonds by challenging each other, women build them by finding similarities.

41. What do you pretend you are asking for in order to sound calm when speaking in PowerPhrases?

   Pretend you are asking someone to pass the butter.

42. In what kinds of situations is silence golden?

   1. It doesn't matter that much.

   2. You are too triggered to speak rationally

   3. Your words are unlikely to bring a good result.

43. What is the e-mail address to send your PowerPhrases questions and PowerPhrase success stories?

   Questions@SpeakStrong.com

   Success@SpeakStrong.com

A Final Personal Note

It has been many years, many negotiations, many confrontations, and many communications since my first wake-up call regarding my need for PowerPhrases. Many personal tests have been passed and some failed—but I assure you, my Personal PowerPhrase GPA has been consistently on the rise.

Communication skills do not solve all problems, but, oh, what a difference they make! Changing habits and testing new waters requires perseverance and courage. They are worth every bit of effort they require.

So stand up, power up, and SpeakStrong. The next time you get wind of a backstabber, address it. When your boss volunteers your department for another project, speak up about the challenges it presents and what you need to meet the challenges. When someone puts you down, tell him how you want to be treated. When someone goes out of her way to help you, let her know exactly why you appreciate it. Take yourself off mute and speak!

Your words become your actions. Your actions shape your destiny. Use PowerPhrases to talk the walk YOU want.

Index

Absolutes, speaking in, 28
Absolute Vicious Venom Poison
      Phrases, 28
Accusations, 130, 163
Acknowledgment, 8
   of participation, 175–176
   of perspective, 156–157
   in saying no, 118
Actions, backing words up with,
      66–69, 97, 113
Active listening, 124–131
Agenda
   avoiding sneaking own in, 126
   hidden, in questions, 145
Aggressive communicators, 207–
      208
   number of words used by, 14,
      167
Aggressive Negative Respect-
      Robbing Phrases, 28–29
Anger, as secondary emotion, 171
Anger, defusing, 156–163
   brevity in, 158
   clarity in, 160–162
   goals in, 159–160
   specificity in, 158–159
   tone in, 162–163
Anger, expression, 164–174
   brevity in, 166–167

Anger, expression (*cont.*):
   clarity in, 169–170
   empty phrases in, 171–173
   goals in, 168–169
   specificity in, 167–168
Answers, asking good questions to
      get, 138–147
Apologizing, 132–137
   brevity in, 133
   goals of, 134–135
   sincerity in, 135–137
   specificity in, 133–134
   tone in, 137
Appreciation, showing, 3, 5, 8
Argument, negative Poison
      Phrases in starting, 30
Artificial barriers, dropping, 89
Assertions, backing up, 93
Assertiveness
   in addressing issues, 185–192
   in responding to put-downs,
      151–152, 155
Assumptions
   avoiding, 49–50
   veiled, 31–32
Attention span, 45–46
Attitude. *See also* Tone
   eliminating, 72–73
   as problem, 58–59

Backing off, at first sign of resistance, 6–7
Backstabbers, addressing, 3
Balance, finding, in communication, 9–10
Balance of power, 11
Blame, 33, 130, 163
  eliminating, 71–72
  in expressing anger, 173–174
Brevity
  in addressing issues, 188
  in communicating feelings, 100–101
  in defusing anger, 158
  in expressing anger, 166–167
  in expressing opinion, 91–92
  in gender communication, 195–196
  in handling disagreements, 176–177
  listening and, 125–126
  in making requests, 108–109
  in perfecting connections, 82–84
  of PowerPhrase questions, 139–140
  of PowerPhrases, 13–14, 43–48
  of response to put-downs, 150–151
  in saying no, 117
Bullying, 161–162

Clarifying questions, 128
Clarity
  in addressing issues, 191
  in communication, 15
  in defusing anger, 160–162
  in expressing anger, 169–170
  in expressing feelings, 104–105
  in expressing opinions, 95–96
  in gender communication, 199–201

Clarity (*cont.*):
  in perfecting connections, 87–89
  in saying no, 118, 120–122
Closed-ended questions, 144
Comebacks to put-downs, 150–151
Communication
  clarity in, 15
  effective, 11
  facing challenges in, 4–5
  of feelings, 99–106
  finding balance in, 9–10
  method of, 207–208
  need-to-know basis for, 195
  Runion Rules for, 211–212
  taking responsibility for, 143–144
  tone in, 16
Complaining, 66–67
Concerns, addressing directly, 32
Conciseness, 44
Conclusions, drawing, 31–32
Condescension, 12–13
Connection, PowerPhrases to perfecting, 81–89
  brevity in, 82–84
  clarity in, 87–89
  goals in, 85–87
  specificity in, 84–85
  tone in, 89
Conversation
  questions to regain control of, 145
  starting and holding, 81–85
"Coulda's," 25
Counter-attacks, 155
Covey, Stephen, 55, 133
Coworkers, questions about dealing with, 216–218
Credibility, 97
  loss of, 18, 69

Criticism
  avoiding, 97
  PowerPhrases responses to un-
    kind, 148–155
Cursing, 168

Defensiveness, 97–98, 103–104,
    127
  avoiding, 58
Details
  avoiding, 100–101
  being precise in, 48–54
  eliminating irrelevant, 45–46
Directions, giving, 46
Disagreements, PowerPhrases in
    handling, 175–184
  brevity in, 176–177
  goals in, 178–181
  specificity in, 177–178
  subjectivity in, 181–182
  tone in, 183–184
"Don't," 29

Effectiveness, 60
Emotions, describing specific,
    101–102
Empty phrases in expressing
    anger, 171–173
Examples, backing up assertions
    with, 93
Expectations, PowerPhrases and,
    209–210
Explanations, focusing questions
    on, 143

Feel-felt-found formula, in handling
    disagreements, 183–184
Feelings
  communication of, 99–106
  use of, as weapons, 106
Filler Respect-Robbing Poison
    Phrases, 18–19

Fine, Deb, 82
The Fine Art of Small Talk (Fine),
    82
Flattery, 88
Follow through, 63
  in addressing issues, 191

Gender, listening and, 193–203
Gender communication
  brevity in, 195–196
  clarity in, 201
  goals in, 198–199
  specificity in, 196–198
  tone in, 202–203
General words in describing emo-
    tions, 101–102
Genuineness, 88–89
Goals
  in addressing issues, 190
  in apologizing, 134–135
  creating, for listeners, 74
  in defusing anger, 159–160
  in expressing anger, 168–169
  focusing on, 55–60
  in gender communication,
    198–199
  in handling disagreements,
    178–181
  in listening, 124–131
  in perfecting connections, 85–87
  of PowerPhrase questions, 141–
    145
  in PowerPhrases, 14–15
  of response to put-downs, 151–
    152
  rooting out misdirected, 56
  in saying no, 119–120
Groveling, 132–137
Guilt, 171

Habits, changing, 34
Heebner, Lesa, 55

Hidden agenda in questions,
     145
Hints, avoiding, 121
Hit and run tactics, 73–74
Hostile remarks, 164–166
     responding to, 10–11

"I," 33–34
Ideas, belief in own, 19–20
"If-only's," 25
Illustrations, backing up assertions
     with, 93
Indecisive Respect-Robbing Poi-
     son Phrases, 21–24
Ineffective speech, price of, 5
Information
     asking questions to get, 141
     giving little extra, 82–83
     need for specific, 49–50
Integrity of words, 66–69
Interpretation, avoiding, 49–50
Intimidation, tactics of, 147
Invisible barriers, 87–88
Issues, PowerPhrases in address-
     ing, 185–192
     brevity in, 188
     clarity in, 191
     follow-through in, 191
     goals in, 190
     listening in, 191
     specificity in, 188–190
     tone in, 191–192
     word choice in, 191–192

Job requirements, being specific
     in, 52–54
Judgment, 130
     avoiding, in handling disagree-
          ment, 183–184
     eliminating, from your words,
          212
     in expressing anger, 173–174

Labeling, 27–28
Larsen, Linda, 59
Limiting nature of Poison Phrases,
     18–19
Listeners
     asking questions to get in-
          volved, 141
     being considerate of, 97
     considering, in making re-
          quests, 113–115
     creating goals for, 74
Listening
     active, 124–131
     in addressing issues, 191
     brevity and, 125–126
     in defusing anger, 158
     gender and, 193–203
     goals in, 124–131
     sincerity in, 129
     specificity and, 126
     tone and, 130–131
Literalness in male communica-
     tion, 194
Loop, keeping people in, 5, 8–9

Manager, communication as new,
     214–216
Manipulativeness, 146–147
Maybe, use of no and, 122
McGraw, Phil, 178
Meaning, identifying your, 61–65
Media, getting attention from,
     46–47
Messages, weakening of, 17, 18–
     26
Misinterpretation, avoiding, 162–
     163
Mixed messages, 73
Muteness, 9

Need-to-know basis of communi-
     cation, 195

Negative, positive versus in achieving results, 114–115
Negative Respect-Robbing Poison Phrases, 24–25
Negative Vicious Venom Poison Phrases, 28–30
Negativity, 5, 9
Neutral story, 73
Nice, power in being, 70–74
No
  brevity in saying, 117
  clarity in saying, 120–122
  goals in saying, 119–120
  as Poison Phrase, 29
  power of saying, 116–123
  specificity in saying, 118–119
  tone in saying, 122–123
"No comment," use of, as phase, 60
The Number One Secrets of Successful Managers (Pitt), 8

Open ended questions, 86–87, 144
Opinions
  disguising, as questions, 199–201
  expressing, 7–8
  importance of making matter, 90–98

Participation, acknowledging, 175–176
Passive-aggressiveness, 151–152
Passive communicators, 207
  number of words used by, 13–14, 166–167
Passive Negative Respect-Robbing Phrases, 28–29
Performance reviews, 9–10
  PowerPhrases in, 219–220
Perfume, sensitivity to, 217–218

Perspective
  acknowledgment of, 156–157
  hearing, 182–183
Persuasion, 90
Pitt, Hal, 8
Playfulness, 88
Points, scoring, 211
Poison Phrases, 17–34, 71
  beginning with "you," 72
  eliminating, 33–34
  Respect-Robbing, 17, 18–26, 63, 167, 207
  Vicious Venom, 17, 27–34, 63, 154, 179, 208
Politicians
  communication by, 61
  loss of credibility by, 69
Positive, versus negative in achieving results, 114–115
Pot-shots, responding to, 153–154
Power, balancing, 212
Powerless words, 25
Power letter, 70
"A PowerPhrase a Week" (e-mail newsletter), 213
PowerPhrase questions
  brevity of, 139–140
  goals of, 141–145
  specificity of, 140–141
PowerPhrase Quiz, 35–39
PowerPhrases
  asking questions with, 138–147
  in balancing workload, 221–223
  brevity of, 13–14, 43–48, 82–84, 91–92, 100–101, 108–109, 117, 125–126, 139–140, 150–151, 158, 166–167, 176–177, 188, 195–196
  clarity in, 15, 87–89, 95–96, 104–105, 120–122, 160–

PowerPhrases (*cont.*):
162, 169–170, 191, 199–201
defined, 13
expectations and, 209–210
in gaining respect, 220–221
gender and, 193–203
goals of, 14–15, 56, 74, 85–87, 119–120, 124–131, 134–135, 141–145, 151–152, 159–160, 168–169, 178–181, 190, 198–199
in handling disagreements, 175–184
to perfect the connection, 81–89
in performance reviews, 219–220
personal note about, 75–77
specificity in, 14, 48–54, 84–85, 92–93, 101–102, 109, 118–119, 126, 133–134, 140–141, 158–159, 167–168, 177–178, 188–190, 196–198
success stories in using, 219–223
as targeted, 14–15, 55–60, 85–87, 94–95, 102–104
tips for using, 207–213
tone in, 12–13, 15, 16, 89, 106, 113–115, 122–123, 130–131, 137, 162–163, 183–184, 191–192, 202–203
truth of, 61–65
use of, 3–4
PowerPhrases Final Exam, 224–238
Power Tips (Larsen), 59
Preciseness in details, 48–54
Priorities, keeping straight, 59–60

Problem, taking ownership of, 33–34
Process, updating people on, 5, 8–9
Profanity, 52
Prophecy, 90
Purposefulness, conveying, 44
Put-downs, 3, 148–155, 159
brevity of response to, 150–151
goals of response to, 151–152
specificity of response to, 151

Qualifier Respect-Robbing Poison Phrases, 19–20
Qualifiers, 98
avoiding, 94, 95
Questions
asking with PowerPhrases, 138–147
clarifying, 128
closed-end, 144
disguising opinions as, 199–201
hidden agenda in, 145
open ended, 86–87, 144
problem of multiple tied together, 139–140
set-up, 146–147

Reasons, giving brief, to support your opinions, 92–93
Refusals, 116–123
Regret in saying no, 122–123
Rejection, 130, 171
Repetition, 213
Requests, 107–115
brevity in making, 108–109
clarity in making, 111–113
considering the listener in making, 113–115
getting results with, 110–111
saying no to, 119
specificity in making, 109

Requests (*cont.*):
    statements as opposed to, 111–113
    tone in, 113–115
Resistance, backing off as first signs of, 6–7
Respect, PowerPhrases in gaining, 66–69, 220–221
Respect-Robbing Poison Phrases, 17, 18–26, 63, 167, 207
    Filler, 18–19
    Indecisive, 21–24
    Negative, 24–25
    Qualifier, 19–20
    Tag, 21
Responsibility
    accepting full, 134
    taking, for communication, 33–34, 143–144
Results
    focusing on, 55–60
    getting, with requests, 110–111
    positive versus negative in achieving, 114–115
Runion Rules for communication, 211–213

Sarcasm, avoiding, 73, 74, 115, 150, 208, 211
Screaming, as inappropriate, 9
Self-disclosure, 147
Self-esteem, 148–155
Self-knowledge, 64–65
Sensitivity, 89
Set-up questions, 146–147
The 7 Habits of Highly Effective People (Covey), 133
"Shoulda's," 25, 30–31
Sideswipes, 73, 154
Silence
    as golden, 5–6, 208–209
    regretting, 5–9

Sincerity
    in apologizing, 135–137
    in listening, 129
Slang, 52
Small talk, 81–89, 94
Speaking freely, 124–131
Specific information, giving, 48–54
Specificity, 14, 48–54
    in addressing issues, 188–190
    in apologizing, 133–134
    in communicating feelings, 101–102
    in defusing anger, 158–159
    in expressing anger, 167–168
    in expressing opinion, 92–93
    in gender communication, 196–198
    in handling disagreements, 177–178
    listening and, 126
    in making requests, 109
    in perfecting connections, 84–85
    of PowerPhrase questions, 140–141
    of response to put-downs, 151
    in saying no, 118–119
Speech
    importance of, 5–9
    patterns of, 5
    price of ineffective, 5
Statements, as opposed to requests, 111–113
Straightforwardness, 62
Subjectivity, in handling disagreements, 181–182
Success stories, 219–223
Suggestions, offering, 7–8
Summaries, with supportive documentation, 92
Supportive documentation, summaries with, 92

Tag phrases in saying no, 118
Tag Respect-Robbing Poison
        Phrases, 21
Tannen, Deborah, 194
Targeting of PowerPhrases, 14–
        15, 55–60, 85–87, 94–95,
        102–104
Tentativeness, 18
Thoughts, paying attention to
        your, 85
Tone, 106. *See also* Attitude; De-
        fensiveness
    in addressing issues, 191–192
    in apologizing, 137
    clarity in, 15
    in communication, 16
    condescending, 12–13
    in defusing anger, 162–163
    in gender communication,
        202–203
    in handling disagreements,
        183–184
    listening and, 130–131
    in perfecting connections, 89
    in requests, 113–115
    in saying no, 122–123
Trust, gaining, in handling dis-
        agreements, 183
Truth
    importance of telling, 5, 6–8
    in PowerPhrases, 61–65
    telling, 152–153
Truth in advertising, 89
Twenty-four hour rule, 105–106,
        212

Vague Hinting Poison Phrases, 26
Vague words, 14
Veiled assumptions, 31–32
Verbal litmus test, 212
Vicious Venom Poison Phrases,
        17, 27–34, 63, 154, 179,
        208
    Absolute, 28
    Negative, 28–30
Visualization, 55
Vulnerability, 161

Williamson, Marianne, 55
Words
    backing up, with actions, 66–
        69, 97, 113
    choice of, 14
        in addressing issues, 191–
        192
    eliminating judgment from,
        212
    general, in describing emotions,
        101–102
    integrity of, 66–69
    powerless, 25
    protecting the integrity of, 66–
        69
    vague, 14
Workload, PowerPhrases in bal-
        ancing, 221–223
"Woulda's," 25

"You" in beginning Poison
        Phrases, 72
"You know" phrase, 21

About the Author

Meryl Runion (Meryl@SpeakTall.com) is an internationally known speaker and trainer whose clients include IBM, Lockheed Martin, the FBI, Army Intelligence, and Bell South. She is a graduate of Vanderbilt University and has a master's degree in the Science of Creative Intelligence. She has been featured in articles in publications such as *USA Today, Woman's World, Women in Business Magazine,* and *Conventions South.* She is a conflict management and communications expert and is available for convention keynotes and executive coaching.

To inquire about booking Meryl for your next event, contact:

American Training Associates (512) 346-9277,

Brooks International Speakers Bureau (303) 825-8700,

Convertion Connection (800) 443-9979, or

Five Star Speakers Bureau (913) 648-6480

To inquire about executive coaching, e-mail Meryl@Howto SayIt.com.

The Simple Truth Solution
A PowerPhrase® a Week!
Say What You Mean, Mean What You Say, Get What You Want!

(Sample Issue)

The Simple Truth in Customer Care

Jan knew there was much at stake in how she handled her angry customer. When his language became "colorful"-so *colorful that Erin Brokovich would have blushed*-Jan told him:

- **I care very much about your problem. When you speak to me in this way I find it difficult to focus on a solution.**

Her customer calmed down and the problem was resolved.

Simple Truth Power Quote of the Week

❝ If your conscious mind does not choose the goal of a conversation, your unconscious mind will! ❞
—Meryl Runion

Poison Phrase of the Week

It would have been the perfect line to use on the man who seemed to think what he had to say was more important than anyone else.

- Will you allow me to be the first person in the room who completes a sentence today?

Sarcasm undercuts trust. To speak the simple truth you must cultivate trust. Even if your sarcasm seems well deserved and even if it gets results, resist the temptation. Finishing your sentence isn't worth stooping to sarcasm, and PowerPhrases always work better. A simple:

- **Excuse me, I wasn't done yet.**

-is the better option.

Simple Truth Success Story

I live "down under" in New Zealand. I already have a copy of the book and I follow the newsletter with great interest. I notice that a great many of your subscribers have difficulty with complainers. So did I. I tried to be sympathetic but ended up listening for hours. If only they would talk about solutions instead of the problem! It was then that I started asking a real PowerPhrase question:

- **"What solutions have you thought of so far?"**
Hey presto! It refocuses their attention!

Send your Success Stories to: Success@SpeakTall.com

Sign up today for your free
"The Simple Truth Solution: *A PowerPhrase® a Week!*" Newsletter!
Send your requests to: Subscribe@SpeakTall.com